CABINCRAFT
and
OUTDOOR LIVING

by

Conrad Meinecke

Author of "Your Cabin in the Woods"

Illustrated by

Victor Aures

GREEN
POINT
BOOKS

For information, address:
Greenpoint Books, Ltd.
767 South 4th Street
Philadelphia, PA 19147
info@greenpointbooks.com

Paperback: 979-8-88677-038-4
Cloth: 979-8-88677-039-1

Cover design
by Michael Schrauzer

Dedicated

to

MY FAMILY

of

WILDWOOD CAMPERS

Preface

In my previous outdoor book, YOUR CABIN IN THE WOODS, I invited letters from my readers to share with me their experiences in cabin lore. I did this because an exchange of cabin lore might build an exchange of ideas. The cabin-in-the-woods idea seemed to strike a note of common interest. I have received letters from all over the world. They were all kindly letters, but not on cabin lore. To my great amazement most writers asked, "Where and how can I find security and retreat from this hurly-burly rushing, and seemingly unsafe world?"

There seems to be a deep, fearful desire to escape — escape from frustrations beyond our control. I think a really wholesome escape, if I may use that term — an escape to run from the crowded city lot to a place where one could plant a garden, raise chickens, pigs and the like — might perhaps add to the national wealth as well as our own good.

To many of us, it appears, our world is a swiftly floundering universe. The war has left unrest . . . Europe starving, wage disputes in America. Here nearly two years after World

War II we were still being rationed on simple things as sugar, butter, soap and many other items; prices soaring, the low-income man trying against odds to make ends meet. Fear, too, deep fear of another war — the atomic age — "Where can I run for safety?"

Well, Brother, it's really a good world. We need to hold steady. A cabin-in-the-woods will give us surcease and release, if we are willing to do a bit of honest hard work on our own to make our own way. This will be the national way, if we all pull at the wheel toward national security. It's a matter of rolling up our sleeves and doing something about it.

Security, after all, is on one's mind. I have found, however, a trip to the woods, a week-end or holiday, always gives me a recharging, a rested viewpoint and, on returning to the job in the city, the world's problems do not seem so severe. I think going to the woods helped me to find not only peace, and courage to carry on, but also the quieting influence of God.

And so I have given these pages (I hope) a buoyant note of what the outdoors has to offer — outdoor cooking, cabin designs, outdoor fireplaces, winter sports — a bit of the art of living in the Great Out Doors.

This is a good world and it will be just what we make of it. God's world never changes.

CONRAD E. MEINECKE.

Contents

Introduction

"STEP INTO MY CABIN"

Introduction

"STEP INTO MY CABIN"

Hi, Brother, welcome to my new cabin. When you come to see me in so wild a setting, I know you, too, must be a lover of the Great Out Doors. Since you come to chat with me about life — the simple, primitive outdoor things and living — then I know that you are a pioneer American at heart.

It's a chill night. Hang up your coat and draw up to the fire. I'm glad you came to talk some more. You ask me why we are still pioneer Americans at heart? Well, Brother, sit back and make yourself comfortable. You have asked a question I have long wanted to discuss. I've asked myself what it was that made our early Americans grow strong; what were the basic principles that helped to build a sturdy and courageous people? I believe millions of Americans are asking these same questions today; for thinking people are concerned — yes, anxious and worried about our future as a nation and what each of us can do to help.

Well, let's go back. What did those early settlers want, hope for, when they cast their lot with this land of promise? What did they

*Fore and hind
foot tracks of
Red Fox.*

Fore and hind
Foot tracks of
Skunk

think this new land could give them that had
been denied them in the "old country?" I'm
sure they said, "I want to live a life that may be
rich, reasonably secure, free from fear of oppression — life that shall find real happiness to
balance the hours of drudgery, the constant
denials and hardships."

We know they wanted to enjoy in the fullest sense, "Liberty" — that golden word which
lured thousands to these shores where the
promise of being a free man was sweeter than
life itself. These men were not mere adven-
turers. They were intrigued with the great
idea of life and liberty. Here was a chance for
a man with initiative and imagination to build
his fortunes. Here, unhampered, he might
bring to his loved ones more of the fruits of
good living.

Our desires are not so different today. Can
we wrest from this land these same values? To
me, the answer is as simple today as it was then.
Since the beginning of time man has sought un-
consciously the freedom in his soul to do what he
pleased and do it unhampered — to live life in
its grandest and fullest measure — to be free
to live that life unfettered by outside domina-
tion. Of course, we learned to understand these
privileges when we learned to respect our
neighbor's property rights and other sacred
rights which today we catalogue as the "Freedom From the Four Fears."

To really achieve the full life and the
freedom of being today, we needs must work

4

for it. Sharing liberty we may indulge in (1) free enterprise — that is, to start off on our own and make a living for ourselves and our loved ones; (2) willingness to work hard to achieve these ends; (3) thrift — that golden quality that is too fast disappearing from nations of people who seem to think there is always plenty; (4) a great and sound faith in God and a working relationship with Him that gives peace of mind.

Here we have it, then — Free Enterprise, Willingness to Work, Thrift and Conservation of Natural Resources, and A Working Fellowship with God. These were basic in those days, fundamental, the door to a golden age. These values remain basic today. Here is a philosophy that welled from the springs of human longing to discover in America the promised land. It attracted, from the four corners of the earth, oppressed people who still had a song in their hearts and believed they could make it vocal. Its melody was liberty. Its rhythm was life.

In those limited days the one source of wealth lay in the land, the good earth. Men planted their feet firmly in the land and the land gave them strength. From the land they built a rich America.

We have many and varied opportunities today, but I still believe that men must again get their feet back in the good earth — be it ranch, farm, half-acre or backyard. Produce wealth out of the good earth, and a new way of life will be born. It is still the sure way to help

Fore and hind foot tracks of Raccoon

Squirrel Tracks

us maintain the basic principles that have made America great. It will keep America great.

Personally, I believe we will yet trek from the big cities back to the country. There will be smaller cities wherein smaller factories may employ five hundred or a thousand men who, after the day's work is over, may quickly return to their homes and garden plots — men who, through eight tedious hours of screwing on nuts and bolts, can still find life, liberty and happiness on their own half-acre in the early morning, after supper and weekends.

At heart the American folk are not wrong. They have been led into factories through this industrial age, (great ponderous machines that must be served), and so living has been in herds, slum. Relaxation has also become machine-made movies, pin ball or card games night after night. Our purposes have become dim and shadowy; but I see on every hand folk who are remembering. They are reverting to the land. To them the land will give its sunshine, its fresh, clean air, its promise of new life and growth. The good earth is our heritage and our future.

Your Family Camp on Wheels

V. Aures

Your Family Camp on Wheels

Assuming that you have an automobile, assuming that you are an unlucky devil who gets but two weeks' vacation — let's put it in reverse — a two weeks' vacation with pay implies you have a steady job, that you are a lucky devil with a job and a two-weeks' vacation with pay,—you want to make that vacation a delight and real adventure for your growing family. If you use your wits, your initiative and resourcefulness, you can make these two weeks rich, sparkling and satisfying even if your wage is not large. Work should give us something more than just bread. With skillful planning, the zest, the fun, the shared growing experiences of a year's hard work can be climaxed with a larking adventure together, if you would like it, in a gypsy wagon or a family camp on wheels.

A Family Camp on Wheels can be yours for almost a song. Your camp site may be anywhere in North America — or points beyond. In the United States we may travel from state to state without having to show visa or passport. Innumerable camping grounds are open

9

to the public. Many woodland spots, offering more privacy, are also available to the careful camper. I like to think of Wisconsin with its myriad large and small lakes as the camping playground of America. Then, too, the hundreds of National Parks, from the "friendly Adirondack peaks" to the staggering grandeur of the Rockies — from Maine to Mexico, offer to us all their beauty. Your vacation need not be confined to summer months. "June may be had by the poorest comer," for this country is so large and vast that one may find June weather every month of the year.

Over the past twenty-five years, we have owned the trailer from which these illustrations have been drawn. I have taken my family with me far and wide. First came the heated debate, "Where shall we go?" There was no need to make resort reservations months in advance. We did study geography, interesting places, road maps. The time table need not depend on railroads, conducted tourist schedule nor taxis. Our course was tempered to the time allowed — a month, two weeks, a weekend, and the size of our pocketbook. It didn't cost much more to feed the family enroute than it did at home. There was only one thing to do. We packed our little covered wagon, checking and rechecking lists of food and fixings for comfort, fun, fellowship. We hitched it behind our car. Ready for the road, we were off to a new adventure.

"Believe it or not," my Family Camp on Wheels has spring beds and good mattresses for four persons — yes, even six with a bit more careful packing and an added small tent. It carries complete kitchen gear — pots, pans and dishes, stove, icebox, tools for repairs, portable toilet. Not only these, but a collapsible table with a roll-up top and folding chairs and stools. We have, also, a real shower bath, with adequate privacy. Soap and water are far too cheap for campers to tolerate unclean bodies.

Part of our equipment was a shovel, rake, broom and pickaxe — all small. We must keep compactness in mind. While we started out with pie tins for plates, tin cups, etc., we finally improved our kitchen and saved space with nesting aluminum. Four pots nested into one another — containing four soup bowls, cups, knives, forks ad spoons. This group rested on four plates nested into two skillets. The entire unit fitted into a waterproof canvas bag and took less space than a water pail. Our stove and reflector oven collapsed into a flat package. With four pairs of busy hands the whole camp could be set up in less than thirty minutes. We made a game of it — improving our setting-up record as you would improve your golf score.

Of course, packing four persons into this little "hotel" was a bit intimate, but usually it was a family circle. Let's not forget that our "living room" and "play room" and (on pleasant days) our "dining room," were the whole outdoors. Even on rainy days when our table was set back under the small canvas porch, and we were dressed in boots, raincoats and hats, there was room to stretch and play beyond and around our tent.

Where shall we go this time? That all adventurous question! Suppose it were a lovely week-end in early fall or spring, when an extra Saturday or Monday was available. We'd have studied the county geodetic maps which revealed the contour lines and pointed out rugged rolling country with large and small

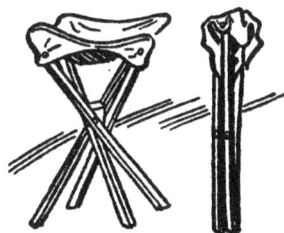

13

streams. We'd trail along the concrete highway and then choose an intriguing dirt crossroad which our map had shown led to some such wild spot. Farmers who have settled in these solitudes are usually friendly folk who enjoy the surprise of a contact with the outside world. "Sure, you can camp in our orchard. Drive right down the lane. Anything you want?" I have always preferred to pay for this privilege. Most often a dollar would be ample. The farmer, too, would gladly sell us vegetables and eggs, and his wife a loaf of homemade bread. You are pretty sure, too, to have a return invitation if you have been a good tidy camper.

So we'd drive in, choose the apple orchard if there was one, strip the waterproof canvas cover from the trailer top, open out the double bed-springs, erect the canvas tent over them, anchor the fly. The stove would be set up in a safe spot, handy to the "dining room" of the moment, yet where the wind would not carry the smoke into the trailer. Soon a bright fire would do its work and savory odors would whet the appetites of the rest of the workers who were setting up the shower bath. It was a simple contraption, this shower bath. A five-gallon collapsible canvas bucket into the bottom of which had been set a spigot. (You can secure this at any hardware store — the kind to which you can attach a bathroom hose and sprinkler.) A rope was tied to the bucket handle. The other end of the rope was slung over the branch of a tree about seven feet from

14

the ground. A strip of canvas, six feet high and about ten feet long, could be strung around the bucket for privacy. A small box for a stool, soap and towel; the bucket filled from the pail now steaming gently over the fire and "Your bath, Sir, is ready." This is the life, and no six-dollar-a-day for room and bath.

Of course, I haven't mentioned in my preoccupation with this refreshing finale before dinner that the bedding had been tucked in over the mattresses (always held in place for traveling by straps), that the icebox had been snuggled into a shady hole and the toilet set out of sight, the lanterns filled and hung to thwart the twilight and the table top set onto is frame and centered with leaves, blossoms and berries.

One year I had the rare privilege of a two months' vacation. We decided to go south. We took our two daughters out of school for February and March and traveled from our home in New York State to Florida and back. The school principal agreed with us that the youngsters could learn more of geography, history, life and people than in a year of school days.

We decided that the fun should begin from the moment we left home behind us. So often it is possible to spoil the present by rushing to a given destination, with no sense of

leisurely discovering the fun and knowledge to be had along the way. The person at the wheel is so often to blame for this rushing and fast driving. Why will some men have such perverse notions! I'm really talking about myself and some things I had to learn to provide riding comfort and true enjoyment. I finally got over trying to pack a month's travel into two weeks. A little paper and pencil work was needed. Three thousand miles packed into ten days would require seven hours of steady driving with an average of forty miles per hour. This would mean holding close to fifty m.p.h. to maintain a forty-mile average. If you want to make a long rush trip, then you won't enjoy your covered wagon or trailer. I learned, too, that the Family Camp on Wheels is best at thirty-five m.p.h. which provides opportunity for all to enjoy the countryside, historical markers and an occasional stop for points of interest. Someone in the car remarks there is a sign-post ahead, looks like the marker of a historic spot, but father having gotten his car to that fifty-five or sixty mile tempo of speed, swishes by and then says apologetically, "Well, that's too bad. I couldn't slow up in time." Then he resumes his same safe and sane driving—50-55-60. Along at three o'clock in the afternoon mother remarks casually, "Let's stop at the next farm where there is a vegetable stand." Soon we come to one, but again father, who seems by now to have but one focus point, the destina-

tion three thousand miles away, drives on. The family yells in unison, "Here are vegetables!", but, alas, father with foot deep on the gas pedal, swishes by again — and again says he is sorry. We then drive the next hundred miles with no vegetables offered for sale. True, we made another added hundred miles today. It's now near seven o'clock. Kiddies, weary and hungry, and mother — well it just isn't fun. We compromise by eating at a "dog" stand, find a place to set up our camp — any place, anywhere — just so we can go to bed. We are weary. So (reward for his pressure driving), the family remains in the car as the chill of the night comes. Father sets up his clever little "Family Camp on Wheels" by himself in the dark. Where did I leave the flashlight?

A Family Camp on Wheels should mean more than a place to sleep. It's what the name implies and so I recommend this kind of trailer for longer encampments and shorter hauls. I have learned, too, for mental happiness and maximum of camping fun: stop driving at three in the afternoon and set up camp. Take time to set up properly near a brook or stream. Enjoy the fun of preparing an outdoor meal.

17

Indeed, the place of your choosing may be so ideal that you may decide to spend a few days. Why not be sufficiently mentally carefree to re-act to this kind of adjustment?

After many trailer trips we actually added a small row-boat or dinghy, 9 ft. long, 3½ ft. beam, a small outboard motor, and a surf board. No, I'm not bragging. The surf board was rigged up from an old woodshed door, but it worked wonderfully. The board, motor and surf board idea came about when we had the two months in Florida. We envisioned ourselves within the sound of the ocean surf on a sandy beach. We dreamed of the early morning dip in the ocean, but no such luck. Choice sandy beach spots were privately owned and public beaches were controlled by local "City Fathers." Those with trailers were politely told of the city block set aside for trailer campers and the law forbade any other camp spots. The city lot for trailer campers is well set-up — usually electric lights with central shower baths and washrooms and other accommodations, but more congested than our closely populated city homes. We did find seclusion by renting a two-acre orange grove for almost a song ($15.00 per month) — just two miles from the ocean. And so we had the privacy we wanted and yet all the ocean bathing and surf-boat riding. No one aboard the "swanky" launches, nor atop the curved commercial surf boards learned more of balance and grace, or had more fun in and out of the waves than did my small daughters. It was satisfying to see them swaying, winging or diving into the wake; swimming strongly until I came around to take them aboard. I was more than content to operate the boat and laugh.

You may now decide "This man is talking about a thousand-dollar venture." Not so fast. I'm a poor man like most people and I wouldn't trade with any man of wealth whose only skill is to make money and buy luxuries. Would two hundred dollars for the outfit I have described seem an orgy of wild spending to get started? Alright then. Let me set out the costs in a bit more detail.

The trailer of the illustration is a commercial product of early vintage. A friend of mine built his own using mine for a model. Through his garage-man he secured axles, three wheels (the third a spare) and springs. He built a box for it four feet by seven by one foot

deep. Attached to each side was a bed spring four feet wide. These were hinged so that they could fold over the box, one upon the other. To each he strapped a mattress. Under the floor of the box he built a cupboard to hold gear and equipment. The canvas tent which folded into the box was an odd shape — twelve feet wide, seven feet deep and seven feet from trailer floor to the peak. Attached to the front was a canvas porch twelve feet wide and seven feet deep. Being handy with tools, he bought the canvas and other material for the inner frame and fashioned his trailer camp during the winter months, in his work shop. Sometimes I think the anticipation is as great as the realization. They certainly go hand in hand. The family share in the planning and in the work. He even rebuilt an old outboard motor, watched for bargains in boats that were sound but needful of paint and patching. His living equipment, like ours, has grown through the years. I am proud of him. Our families spent the next summer vacationing together. He and I sat proudly watching our happy offspring who were finding the fun of God's Great Out Doors —enjoying the fruits of our winter workshop labors. "Well," Bill said to me, "You get out of it just what you put in — yes, with real interest."

"If you didn't have it — this Family Camp On Wheels, what kind of a camp would you most like to have?"

He gave me that classic answer, "I'd have a Family Camp On Wheels." And so would I!

During these twenty-five years with our Family Camp on Wheels we have camped on many lovely camping spots — beside brooks, streams, lakes. Often the family would say after a long week-end in the woods, "Can we buy a place like this?" Well the "miracle" happened — and all within our pocketbook. You, too, can find your dream spot — land for one, five or ten dollars per acre. If too barren, plant trees. They will grow with your love of the place.

We found our spot in the great Zoar Valley near Springville, New York. It is bounded by the on-rushing, swirling Cattaraugus on one side. On the other, encircling woodland hills extend to the skies. It is far too rough for pasture, and with just a bit of river bottom land for gardening. Three babbling brooks slosh and tumble down the wooded slopes. Hemlock aplenty for real log cabins some day. There are wild grapes and berries for the taking. Frogs and frog-legs for dinner. Mint for juleps. Wild roots for salads. Springs for cool drinks. Hickory and walnut trees for nuts and their winter fun. Crabapple and apple trees planted by pioneers of an earlier generation. Here we will trim, graft new life, spray and have perfect apples again.

We have stopped being gypsies. We have taken our beloved Family Camp on Wheels off the highway, recalling the days when it said to us, "Come on. Let's go! I just can't stay folded up," and we didn't talk back, we just packed up and went — to Maine, to Quebec, to Wisconsin, to Carolina.

But we have taken the trailer off the highway. Like the old fire horse, we turned it out to pasture. It now serves as the Guest Camp on our own little Ranch and seems content. Soon we shall build a small cabin. We will build it ourselves, as we built up our trailer equipment.

You, too, may have your Family Camp on Wheels, or your Cabin in the Woods, if such as these are your dreams.

Forest Fires

Forest Fires

Forest fires caused by natural forces can be easily controlled. It is the fires caused by individual carelessness and ignorance that play havoc. Dry leaves and pine needles, inches deep, need but the slightest spark to launch a forest conflagration. Surely a person must be lost mentally and morally if he would deliberately start such destruction. He has never seen the results of fire in a forest — the flight of wild life toward water — water that shrinks with the heat — so that their haven becomes a death trap. He has never seen beautiful proud trees denuded of branches, their trunks living red coals, turning at last to gaunt ghosts in a barren hell of charred death.

The cigarette smoker who carelessly flips his still-glowing butt from a car window, or drops it as he hikes, is a destroyer of life. He loves none but himself. He can be classed with the hunter whose inaccurate aim leaves his prey to run wounded, to die of fever and helplessness and starvation. Leo King, that great Adirondack woodsman, shocked me once when we were in the woods together. As he finished his

cigarette down to the last half-inch, he spit in
the palm of his hand and dipped the still glowing stub into the spittle, rubbing it into noth-
ingness before he was content to throw it away.
Not a tidy procedure this? This man had once
been driven before a forest fire. He had been
burned in fighting forest fires. He knew and
was protecting the life and forests he loved.
God give us more men as thoughtful.

The casual camper is another menace to
our forests. Be sure to put out your fire,
Brother! If you cannot find a rock for a base,
or an open spot away from deep vegetation,
then do a bit of digging and have on hand
buckets of water to soak the ground under-
neath. Better still, if you are not woods wise,
build no fire in the woods, but resort to public
parks where outdoor fireplaces are provided.

Life

Life

"I want free life and I want fresh air," wrote Frank Desprez. This poet has put it into a nutshell. The words, "free life" as against a regulated, controlled, hampered life.

Life is mine for the seeking. I've always wanted in life to have a cabin in the woods and reasonable time to play in it without asking any man's permission. I found the land and I built my own cabin just as I wanted it. It's a simple little cabin, but it's my own. Occasionally I want to go fishing or camping with the family. I want friends to come to my house and I want them to ask me and mine. I want a home for my family to grow up in. I want to have courage enough to assume a small mortgage and the stable qualities to pay for it in the course of fifteen or twenty years. I want a happy home that is my castle, where my children may romp and play. I never did like landlords and therefore preferred my own simple home to a more swanky apartment. My grandson, who lived with us during the war days, had a dog, a cat, a caged bunny and a dozen neighborhood youngsters in his small backyard play-lot, which

I built for him, to give him a normal daily program until his daddy returned.

I want a savings account — small — but sufficient to give me assurance that I can pay the extra doctor or hospital bill when due. I want a bit of cultural life for my family and myself; an occasional good movie, the theatre, the concert. I want a bit more education for my children than I had and want to save consistently against the time, either by long-term insurance or plain monthly savings. I want at least one long trip or journey far from home for every member of the family — this tempered, of course, by my ability to produce and save.

Years ago when my wife and I established our home and family, we searched earnestly for a formula, a philosophy of life that would give us and our children a balanced concept of life that would help us and them to grow strong and be worthy Americans. We wanted them to find and capture stamina and poised resilience that would withstand the test of trial and temptation. We wanted to help them build their own working philosophy in which we no longer needed to guard them from the temptation of life, but to set them free to penetrate the vicissitudes of life and still hold to their own wholesome pattern of living. It's our job, as parents, to let go as fast as our youngsters take hold with understanding and judgment. The formula has served us well. It came out of early America — the search for Life and Liberty.

How often have we heard parents say: "I don't want my children to labor for education or achievement as I did." They want to make it easier for their offspring. Dear parents, by the very struggle you grew strong and generous. Struggle, a bit of privation, hard work well balanced with fun and cultural values, will help your sons and daughters to grow strong. My neighbor paid six hundred dollars a year on his son's university education. He said, "It's up to Bill to earn the other four hundred each year." "Silver platter" gifts just will not end in "clouds with silver linings."

The wage earners, tied to the city with their families of three, five or seven, living on a thirty-foot city lot and working alone to support their growing family, have tough going. There are no real jobs for a city boy or girl. True, some carry papers, shovel snow for pay or share a bit the fringes of home jobs in which they have little interest or understanding. As a contrast, the boy on the farm learned not only the discipline of regular daily chores, but sensed that the part he played was related to the duties of others and to the health and wealth of the family. He learned that thrift was important. Broken tools were repaired, not junked or replaced from a nearby hardware store, and too often charged to father.

There is a deeper value that comes from this communal co-operation. It teaches a subtle lesson in sharing, generosity and helpfulness. Having too little to do is often a cruel

factor in a city boy's life. He wants to do increasingly less. He seeks the passive, the amusing, the canned fun produced by someone else. He has no chance to discover the sparkle and promise of an early spring morning. He perhaps needs to be called two, three or four times before he drags downstairs in the morning, sniffs at a breakfast of commercialized vitamins (never knowing that real food comes from the good earth) and dashes belatedly to school without having given of himself except for himself. It is not really his fault that he has grown selfish and self-centered. He has had little chance to practice any other way of living.

On my fourteenth birthday, I shall never forget, after simple gifts and good wishes, my mother said, "You are a year older. You must now take on broader responsibilities." So I had to build the fire each morning in the kitchen stove. The family alarm was entrusted to me. I called father. He roused the rest of the family. Each began appointed tasks. My cousin Lee lived with us. He rebuilt the living-room fire, cleaning and carrying out the wood ashes which were carefully hoarded in the lye vat from which later we drew lye for hominy and homemade soap.

After building the kitchen-stove fire, from firewood and kindling placed ready in the wood box the night before, I put on my heavy jacket, home-knit cap, mittens and muffler and overshoes to begin the outdoor chores. I fed the chickens (two hundred or more), filling their frozen feed pans with fresh warm water. I cleaned out the night's manure from Old Dexter's stall, curried him a bit and left for him fresh hay, grain and water. On the way back to the house I stopped for an armful of wood — for the wood box may never be empty.

Could there ever be a sweeter moment to a hungry boy than the sight and smell of that breakfast — sizzling bacon, sputtering eggs, griddle smoking as it received the rich sourdough! The table laden with butter, maple syrup, cream to temper the large mugs of steaming, fragrant coffee, and centered with a plate of sugar cookies from mother's cookie jar! Reward convincing and immediate for my early rising. Had I failed to build the fire, there would have been a breakdown in the chain of morning events. I remember there were such mishaps until I was disciplined to understand my responsibility in the family scheme of things. I should not call it discipline; perhaps it was positve leadership on the part of my parents — but it was sound and it produced results.

"Free life and fresh air" go well together — the "fresh air" of a freed mind — a mind that can take the measure of the other man and stand up to him — a freed mind that looks on life as something good and worth striving for. I have heard a man say, "Life has been good to me." Well, Brother, I'm sure you

didn't expect something for nothing. You did something about it. It didn't just happen.

What I want in life didn't all come as I wanted, but I'm still a free man in America and it's up to me to make my dreams come true. No man shall stop me!

Your Treasure
Chest

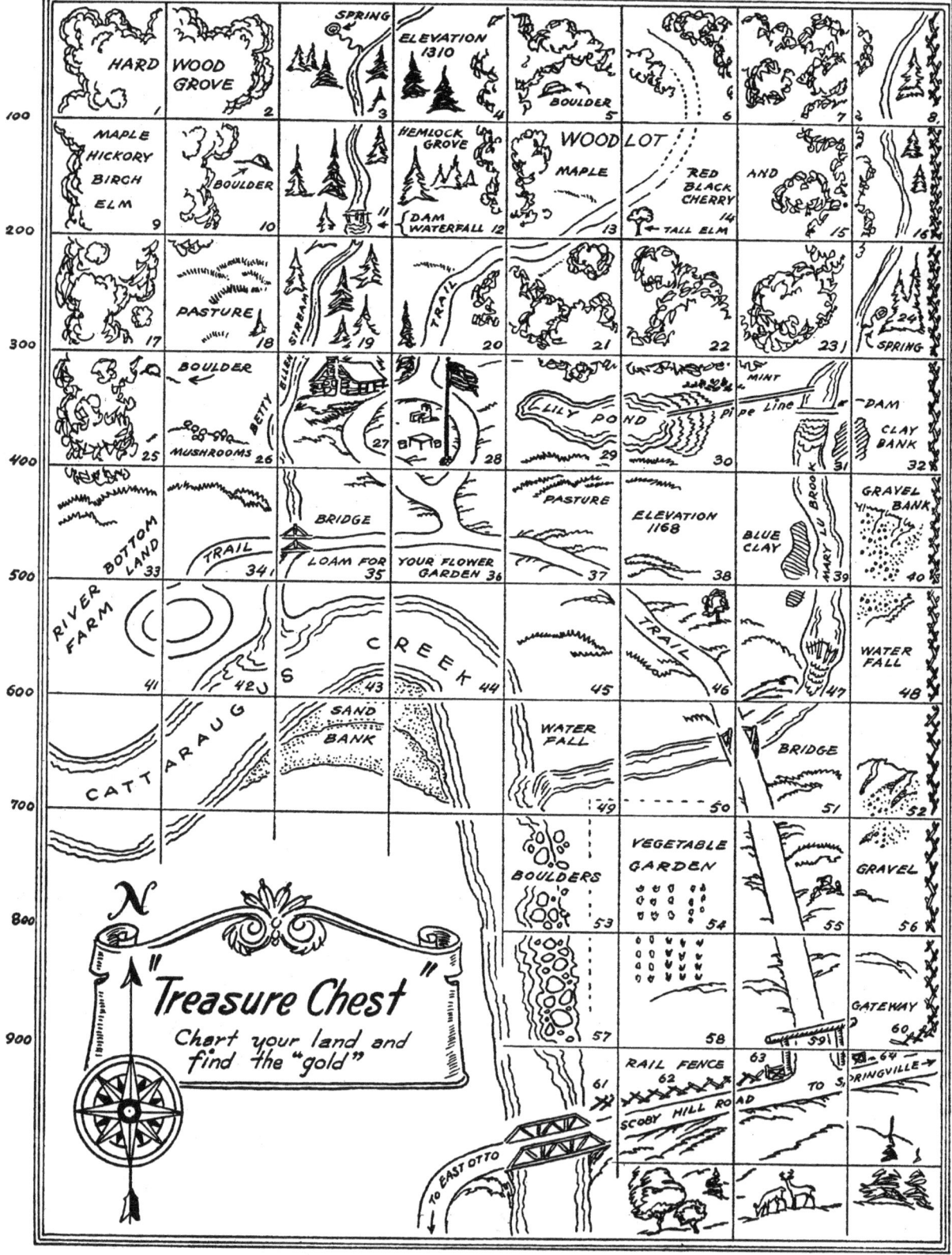

HARD WOOD GROVE 1 2

SPRING 3

ELEVATION 1310 4

BOULDER 5

6 7 8

MAPLE HICKORY BIRCH ELM 9

BOULDER 10

11

HEMLOCK GROVE 12 DAM WATERFALL

WOOD LOT MAPLE 13

RED BLACK CHERRY 14 TALL ELM

AND 15

16

17

PASTURE 18

STREAM 19

TRAIL 20

21

22

23

24 SPRING

BOULDER 25

MUSHROOMS 26 BETTY ELLEN

27

28

LILY POND 29

30

MINT Pipe Line 31 MARY LU BROOK

DAM CLAY BANK 32

RIVER BOTTOM LAND 33

TRAIL 34

BRIDGE LOAM FOR 35

YOUR FLOWER GARDEN 36

PASTURE 37

ELEVATION 1168 38

BLUE CLAY 39

GRAVEL BANK 40

RIVER FARM 41

42

43

CREEK 44

45

TRAIL 46

47

WATER FALL 48

CATTARAUGUS

SAND BANK

49 50

BRIDGE 51

52

BOULDERS 53

VEGETABLE GARDEN 54

55

GRAVEL 56

57

58

59 60

GATEWAY

N

"Treasure Chest"

Chart your land and find the "gold"

61

RAIL FENCE 62

63

64

SCOBY HILL ROAD TO SPRINGVILLE

TO EAST OTTO

100 200 300 400 500 600 700 780

100 200 300 400 500 600 700 800 900

Your Treasure Chest

"There's gold in them thar hills" may be said of your acres. You don't have to be a "Forty-niner," nor travel to the ends of the earth for your "gold." It is on your own land— if you know where to find it. One man turned his gravel hill into a gravel pit that paid him richly. He took toll of each load. Another discovered a clay bank. The blue gravel-free clay was suitable for fine pottery and brought a good price — and a new craft interest. A third chap made capital out of a marshy pond busy with bullfrogs. He supplies a New York market with frog-legs.

Trees planted as seedlings yield a rich return in about twenty years. Plant the type that will grow best on your particular acres. I plant five hundred evergreens each spring on

my land. Now I have a hundred or more eight and ten-foot trees that need thinning. I could sell them for Christmas trees — red pine with its long needles, balsam, white pine, spruce, hemlock, jack-pine, but we will have a Christmas tree party this year for our close friends. They will come out with their kiddies and have the fun of cutting their own holiday trees.

Plant clover — red and white. It will add color to your acres and fragrance, too. Golden honey for winter sweets can be yours if you add a bee-hive or two. Which reminds me that your maple trees will add amber syrup. This is yours for the taking — but that is another story in this book.

Rocks need not be a liability. They are wealth if used for fences, fireplace or other building construction. In the earth may even lie natural gas — and oil. I do not mean to be mercenary, but I do urge that you explore all the possibilities of your acres. If water is available, a sheep, a steer, a goat that gives milk can be fed off the land — adding to your wealth with little of the routine care and housing necessary for chickens, cows, etc.

It is amazing how my little ranch blossoms and prospers each year. As soon as pine, spruce and balsam seedling have developed a sound root base, they seem to jump eighteen to thirty inches each year, stretching skyward a slender spire that soon branches out. Even the forgotten trees and bushes along my fences show lush growth — and behold, the highway,

the passing cars become obscured. Our cabin is not only land-locked, but tree-locked.

I'd like to share with you a device which I have used to help me in the knowledge and use of resources on my land. I have made a master map. On it I have noted the location of hickory, butternut and black walnut trees. Here, too, are spotted a dozen old apple trees and wild-thorn-apple. Upon these may be grafted young apple branches which will bear fruit in a year or two. On the south hillside, just above the early frost line, I have set out a small but varied orchard — apples, plums and cherries. Remember the luscious Russets? They have almost gone out of fashion; but not in my orchard. To change a weed fruit-tree into a bearing fruit of good flavor and size means careful pruning and trimming and then fertilization. I've even fussed with a thorn-apple until its fruit is twice the size of its wild state. Thorn-apples go back to my boyhood days; so I must have a thorn-apple tree.

Let me share with you the secret for finding hidden "treasure" on your acres, the technique of mapping so that you may study your land; be it one acre or a hundred, you must know it.

Test the soil value. Any County Agricultural Agent will help you do this. He will show you how to apply the treatment it needs. Study the sub-strata. A six-foot posthole digger may reveal gravel or springs. Rushes, too, may indicate springs of real value. Running water means that you may have fresh spring greens, watercress and mint for your Mint Julep, and dried spices.

Study every foot of your land and you will discover hidden "gold" which will not require the miner's pick and shovel. Here's how to make the master map of your possible riches.

Let's say you have a sixteen-acre plot. This means about 800 by 800 feet. Start at the upper left corner. Pace off along the fence line a hundred feet. (Establish your own stride. You don't need a tape line. Mine is just $2\frac{1}{2}$ feet to each step.) Plant a stake each hundred feet and repeat the process across the upper land and then down one side. You are designing an exact checker board picture of your land. For true reliability travel the lines down and up with a compass so that your stakes — each four — will form perfect hundred-foot squares that may be represented accurately on a scale map.

Take with you a notebook and pencil. Observe and record everything you see to left and right of your stake lines. Here — in Square No. 10 which would be 200 feet east of starting point and down 150 feet, is a boulder of rich red stone that will be an excellent corner-stone for your cabin fireplace. Or, 250 feet east by 35 feet south, is a trickling spring — or wintergreen berries — or a hickory tree for future funiture. You note that the little brook which flows down to the bottom land will assure you water for a garden regardless of the weather

and could be dammed for a natural pool, or piped across lots for power, craftshop machinery or a fountain forty feet high. (My hills run 300 feet high.)

Now all this may sound a bit complicated. If you like what I have explained so far, let's chart this checkerboard into larger, more easily recognized zones. As you have traversed the land forward and back, you have noted landmarks more easily "picked up" than the 100 ft. stakes. Designate these on your map. This map now holds a place of honor on your cabin wall. To establish markers you may even like to erect a stone pile or cairn marker on each 200 foot corner, if no outstanding landmark is nearby. This may have a name or a number on the master map. Now when you want to relocate the hidden boulder, or the spring with its watercress, it will be an easy matter. A tall maple or a windblown elm may be your marker. You do not know one tree from another? Well, Brother, that makes it doubly interesting for now you may step into a new world — the tree world. Your five-foot book-shelf will soon harbor the best book on "How to identify trees." As your respect grows, your understanding deepens and you realize indeed "only God can make a tree." When this happens you will need a longer bookshelf, for you will want to know the names of the birds you see, the insects that harm and help, the history of the rock structure, the meaning of the color. You will come alive to wild plant life and wonder if

41

these mushrooms and berries are edible. In short, the "gold" will be translated into golden light of new knowledge. You will find a new source of entertainment, of recreation. With a light heart, a grateful heart, you will find the "Golden Age of Life" — the treasure of happiness — all for the taking on your own acres. This is my idea of a paradise on earth.

So, build your master map from your field notes. Search the tree tops. Search the shy wood-life. Search the sub-strata of your land. Your map may lead you to a "buried treasure." Who knows? In this happy health-giving search you will find more than "gold" — you will discover God in the Great Out Doors.

Water

Water

Pure drinking water is as essential as pure air. There is something about spring water that is different from any other form of drinking water. It is refreshingly cool and yet, though one drinks great drafts of it, it is not like ice water in its effect upon one's stomach.

I have a favorite spring to which I trudge a mile just for a deep satisfying drink. The spring forms a deep pool surrounded by moss and rocks. Watercress and fresh greens line the sides of the little stream below. Somehow I grow sentimental and make a ceremony of the approach. To lie flat on one's stomach is not at all undignified — prone, nestling close to Mother Earth — lips touching the sparkling water. I cannot stop there. Face deeper and deeper into the spring, until opening my immersed eyes I behold a new world. The crystal water serves as a magnifying glass, showing the delicate plant life, the bubbling particles of white sand dancing playfully about those small apertures in the earth from which flows this frolicking stream. Then up again for a breath of God's fresh air. And again and again a deep draft. Why must I return to the kitchen faucet to draw a glass of chlorinated, medicated fluid that is hopefully labeled "pure drinking water."

Indian Cucumber

45

WILD
MINT

Life in the outdoors may take the crease
out of a man's trousers, but it will leave impres-
sions of things fundamental, values against
which to judge the shallowness of modern
civilization. A great crony of mine, Samuel
Bogan*, once invited me to his "Hermit's shack"
in Connecticut for a week-end. He waxed
warm about his favorite spring which was nearby. We both went to visit it, to drink deeply
from its cool waters. As we sat there he told me
of its history. I said, "Sam, write what you have
just told me." He did and here it is — a classic legend of an ageless spring in the woods:

"I suppose that most of us are amphi-
bians at heart. We like to rest beside a
flowing stream. We feel, with Seneca,
that 'where the spring rises and the river
flows, there we should build our altars
and offer our sacrifices.' We like rain,
and clear lakes, and mountain brooks that
sing. We like water done up in glaciers,
and the magnificent undrinkable sea.

"When my own spirit is battered and
I am possessed of that indefinable thirst
not quenched by ordinary water, I like to
go to my favorite spring. It lies in the
forest at the foot of a long sweeping hill,
and the water comes from deep rock
crevices. It is a pure spring and its flow
does not change with the seasons. Its
temperature is the same the whole year
round. The pressure of the great hill

*Samuel D. Bogan, author of "Let the Coyotes Howl."

46

pushes the water outward, and the pressure of the water throws up a small fountain of sand. The little grains of clear and milky quartz form a cascade at the bottom of the transparent basin.

"The water is clear, but the spring is not colorless. The adjacent earth and sky hide nothing from it. The sky rests there and the trees are reflected upside-down. It is as though one could reach into the spring and touch the sky, or wrap one's finger in a cloud, or pluck a leaf from the tiny trees. Then, suddenly, like Narcissus, you see your face. Yet, if you look closely at your face in the spring, it shuts out the sky. It is a reminder that 'he who loves himself will have no rivals.'

"The spring, walled in by moss-covered rocks, is as old and as permanent as the contours of the land in which it lies.

"It was formed when the last glacier receded from New England some thirty thousand years ago. This is to realize, with awe, that prehistoric animals have drunk from it.

"Once, in cleaning it out, we found an arrowhead. What Brave left it, and in what year? The pioneers came, too. They lived near, and planted apples and maples. Where did they go and why? Westward, with the Forty-Niners? to the prairies? the wide Pacific?

Curled
Dock

47

"Yesterday, that is to say, only fifty years ago, a hermit built a cabin on the slope and the spring was his for a while and takes its name from him, THE HERMIT'S SPRING.

"The spring is indescribable because, being perfect, it is not supposed to exist. Have we not heard many times that nothing is perfect? But I know better. I have seen the leaves of autumn on this spring, and the pebble-tossing fountain on its floor. I have seen within it the blue inverted sky, and a flight of birds across the sky. I knew that the leaves were perfect, and the fountain, and the sky, but once, when on a clear winter night, I drank from it and suddenly realized that my face was immersed in a cool sky of stars, and my spirit rested for a while. I was not thirsty anymore."

God has provided us with refreshment for our souls, with fresh air and good water, but somehow we are careless in our use and care of them. If you have a spring on your acres, be sure to protect it against contamination. If it is on a hillside, build a ditch above it so that seepage water will be turned aside and there will be no possible polution. I have added to the ditch a protecting fence to keep out wandering animals, a neighbor's cow, or thoughtless visitors unfamiliar with the ways of the woods and the value of natural resources.

chickory

48

The Amateur
Architect

The Amateur Architect

When planning a home of several rooms, in which the cellar, first floor, second floor, attic, (also bath) are involved, one does not save money by being his own architect. But to plan your own cabin-in-the-woods, of one or two or three rooms, by all means be your own amateur architect. Even though you have had no experience, here are some very simple rules and methods to help you. Above all this, you will get a real thrill in doing your own planning.

Cabin planning is different from planning a city home. First of all there is little need for a cellar, so start with a good foundation. So many wood-be cabin builders think they can save money by building a cabin on concrete piers — one at each corner of the cabin. This is getting off to a very bad start. Piers settle until finally the cabin floor is no longer level — cracks appear in the walls and the cabin is no longer snug and tight. A good eight-inch concrete wall all around will prove cheapest in the end. It must go below frost line, i.e., three and a half feet below ground level in New York

State. A twelve-inch footing for the eight-inch wall is desirable.

Let's take, for example, a cabin with combination living room and dining room, porch, kitchen and bath. Size overall, 18'x32'. After the concrete is poured, bury one-half or five-eighth inch bolts in the soft cement. Bolts should be long enough to sink eight inches into the cement and protrude upward to bolt down the first log. (In frame building enough to bolt through two 2x4 sills).

But now let's get back to the floor plan. In these pages you will find many suggestions of cabins, bay windows, rustic doors and windows, built-in features for books, cupboards, nooks, window seats, etc. I have avoided detailed floor plans, for, after all, it should be your cabin, not mine. Your conception of size of rooms will naturally differ from mine. I

do, however, present some methods. Talking towards some simple principles will prove more helpful than trying to tell my reader how to proceed at every step.

Let us then look at the overall picture, from size of cabin to cupboards, furniture — yes, rugs — to fit the plan. How much furniture will be included: beds, tables, cupboards, etc.? How much space will the fireplace take? Doors should be 2′ 8″ wide, by at least 6′ 6″ high. Windows to fit in between, and size to suit one's fancy. Most log cabins are spoiled with small windows. A modern log cabin must have large windows to provide plenty of light. In one of my cabins, which measures 14′x16′, I have an end window measuring 6′x8′ which not only gives a burst of light within, but also provides a beautiful view over the countryside.

CONSIDER EACH SQUARE AS ONE FOOT

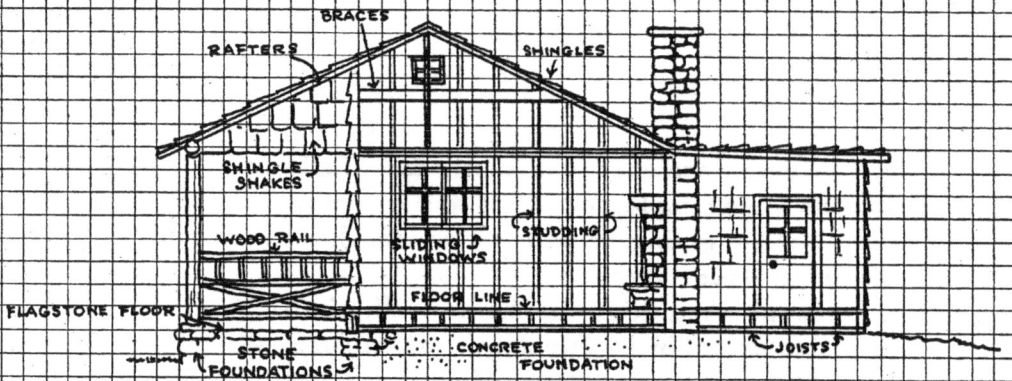

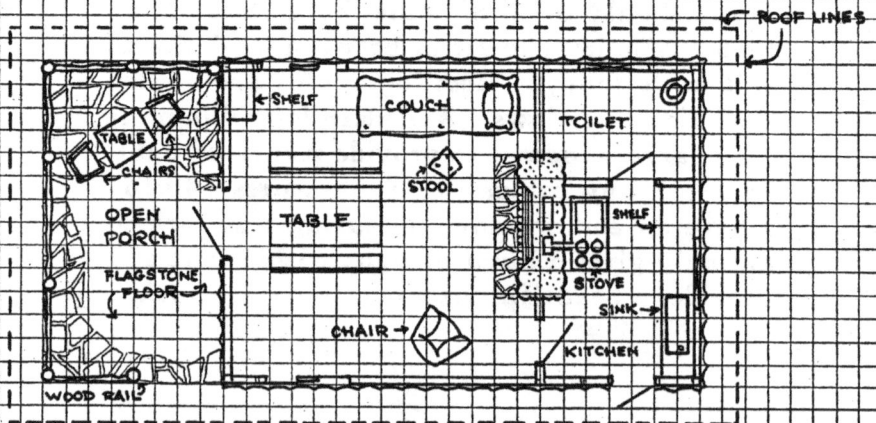

BRACES

RAFTERS

SHINGLES

SHINGLE SHAKES

WOOD RAIL

SLIDING WINDOWS

STUDDING

FLOOR LINE

FLAGSTONE FLOOR

STONE FOUNDATIONS

CONCRETE FOUNDATION

JOISTS

ROOF LINES

SHELF

COUCH

TOILET

TABLE

CHAIRS

STOOL

SHELF

OPEN PORCH

TABLE

STOVE

FLAGSTONE FLOOR

SINK

CHAIR

KITCHEN

WOOD RAIL

The accompanying map of quadrille paper will help to lay out the first floor plan in the most minute detail. Consider each square one foot. It is obvious then if the cabin is to be 32 feet long and 18 feet wide, we need to count the exact number of squares to get a fair picture of the size of the cabin. Just where shall we place the bed and how much space will it take? At this point take a yardstick and measure the bed. Three feet wide by six feet six inches long? Again we count off the same number of squares and will be amazed to find how much space it really takes, in relation to the room itself. If two comfortable lounging chairs are to be included, then measure these, too, and draw them in the floor plan. A fireplace requires about 7 feet by three feet floor space, if you want an open hearth three feet wide. Cupboards, table and other furniture must also be included.

At this point we may find that we need a larger cabin to house all the comforts desired. Remember the man who says after his cabin is finished, "If I were to build again, I'd do so and so . . ." So, Mr. Amateur Architect, you will do well to spend winter evenings in laying out your floor plan on paper. After the floor plan, use again the quadrille paper to plan the side walls, again one square to the foot. Raise or lower the roof to give your cabin graceful lines. Draw in the doors and windows to scale. A log cabin in which the gable is included as part of the main living room, leaves one free to start with lower sidewalls, i.e., a seven-foot sidewall is ample with the roof slanting upward to thirteen, fourteen or fifteen-foot peak, according to one's fancy. When laying out the floor plan, make all measurements starting from the inside of the cabin. Then add the thickness of the walls on the outside. Another common error made in cabin construction is to be skimpy about the over-hanging roof. The cabin here described can well afford to have an over-hang of eighteen inches to two feet, especially on the gable ends.

It has always proved helpful to me, after drawing plans for my cabin construction, to next build a miniature cabin, one inch to the foot. Leave the roof removable. Here is indeed ideal winter "sport", especially if you build all the furniture, cupboards, etc. to scale. I recommend this to the novice in cabin building. It's almost a guarantee against going wrong. Take the miniature along to your cabin spot. You will find yourself familiar with every measurement — exact length of each log, board, fitting.

Of course, the easier way is to hire an
architect and contractor, but more than half of
the fun is building your cabin-in-the-woods,
from the planning to the building it, with your
own hands. It will be really yours. It's what
you put into it of yourself that will really make
it a part of you.

LOGS BEVELED
TOWARD WINDOW

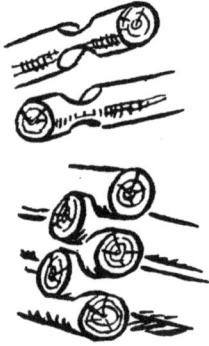

NOTCHING LOGS

Notching logs is a craft one does not learn merely by reading books. Notching logs so that they fit together snugly is an art all in itself. It belongs to the Pioneer Skills, to the Woodsman, to the man intimately acquainted with an axe — more than this, with the broad axe, the pewee, the cant hook.

If you want a cabin true to the Pioneer background, it will be of the notched log construction and you will need to find a backwoodsman who has mastered the art of delicately swinging an axe. He will teach you more in a day than you can learn from a dozen books. As has been said often, "Theory without practice is empty and practice without theory is deadly." Combine the two and you will acquire a technique that is workable. Only then will you be on your own.

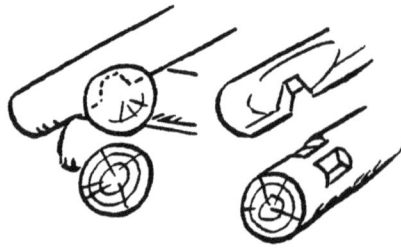

Fireplace Magic

Fireplace Magic

It is a simple thing to talk about a glowing fireplace. To achieve one takes skill, plus a few tricks up your sleeve. The ash bed is important. The kind of wood and the placing of the logs determine your success. The only thermostat is the fire-builder himself. If he learns the secret of its magic, he can make of his firemaking a fine art, shading it, highlighting it, coloring it with craftsmanship that need not depend on chemicals from a package or bottle.

Let's learn the art from scratch. Housewives unacquainted with fireplace craft, will clean out and scour the fire bed, leaving it empty, clean, naked. I have discovered the main reason. They desire a clean and tidy setting. So do I. Ashes can add rather than detract from the beauty and efficiency of your fire. Today we desecrate a fire by throwing into it cigar and cigarette butts, trash, paper. These seldom burn in entirety, and if they do, leave a black char that is most unsightly. It might seem unnecessary to say that food waste should never enter into this symbol of family

61

life. A fireplace that is an incinerator would have to be cleaned. A fireplace that centers the warmth and light and friendliness of a group of fireplace lovers will never be so desecrated.

A fireplace without a deep cushion of ashes is like a bed without a mattress. Ashes form the soft warm bed for the next fire. Without it, the logs won't burn correctly. The mat of ashes should be six inches deep at the back wall of your fireplace. They will be white and clean if you become a master of your art and burn only hard wood.

So, first, as you build your fire, rake the ashes back so that they slant upward from the hearth's front to the six-inch depth at the back of the fire wall. You need no grate or andirons. A bed of ashes is the real need. In the center of your fireplace build a small "tepee" of kindling, dry tindery bits, preferably full of pitch. At right angles, one on either side, lay two three- or four-inch sticks of wood running from front to back. Now lay a thick backlog, say ten inches, way in the back on the sticks; next forward a smaller log in thickness, but not touching. Then a still smaller log and so on to the hearth's edge. Air currents, which create correct draft, travel along the outside or ends of these logs, flowing up and in between them. A diagonal log placed on top of this pile will give added pull to the flame. Your fire is ready for lighting. As the coals form and the under logs burn through and allow the fire to settle into the coal

63

and ash bed, they will not need to be replaced, as the flames themselves give added impetus. If you want your fireplace full of lively flame — I don't mean just a flickering glow, but a burst of light and warmth — continue to add logs diagonally or thrust into the crevices, upright smaller pieces — "ticklers" I call them. Abe Lincoln did his studying by such a light.

Your choice of woods depends upon the purpose and the mood for which the fire is designed. Some woods make a crackling fire. Others throw out showers of sparks. Still others burn slowly and leave a deep bed of coals. Hemlock, pine and other soft woods are good for kindling, but burn out quickly and leave a dark ash. Beech, maple, elm, ash and hickory, are tops. Oak and pitch pine will burn well together. They leave a bed of glowing coals and when spent, a white ash. Any of these hard woods can be used for broiling steaks. A deep bed of coals is essential to any fireplace cooking.

Try birch wood for a fire of welcome. It sputters, crackles, seems to say to your five o'clock tea guest, "Come in. Warm up a bit. Draw up a chair." Birch doesn't last long, but it is sprightly while it burns. I keep a small stock of this rollicking, laughing wood for such special occasions.

Now let me tell you about the choicest of all firelogs, if you want a quiet, colorful fire for the late evening — for the deeper, more silent moods. It neither spits nor sparkles. It throws blue, red, green, yellow and purple flames and all the shades and colors in between. It inspires close companionship. "When a young man's fancy turns to thoughts of love," it is before such a fire he should make his declaration. (It really works.) This special, magic wood is — just your old apple tree from the orchard. It is gnarled, covered with buds, often sprouting twigs. It's a tough old tree. Even when its inside is hollow, it keeps right on growing — giving shade and apples. The very hollowness adds to your fire magic. Set it up, chimney fashion, and watch the glow and constant change of color. Watch the "fire fairies" climb out of its heart and soar upward with the smoke. I sometimes fancy the old tree is remembering and sharing with us the earlier glory of its pink and cream blossoms, the human romances that bloomed in its deep green shade, the fulfillment of its green and scarlet fruit. As a tree, the apple is a romantic, attracting young and old. As firewood, it is an artist of color that warms the hands, the heart — the soul.

The overnight backlog is indeed a part of your fireplace craft. You can keep your log burning all night. If properly buried it will greet you in the morning as a solid log of glowing coals. Just before going to bed take your shovel and rake forward from the back wall of your fireplace, all coals and ashes. Dig down deep through the six inches of ashes, a place to hold a ten-inch log. After dropping the log into this hollow, cover all of it with the rest of your coals and ashes. Bury it until you can see no part of the log for coals and ashes. Now place your screen in front of the hearth for protection from sparks. Behold, tomorrow morning you will find your log of red hot coals. Our pioneer fathers did this always; especially in the days when there were no matches and fires were built by rubbing sticks, or with flint on steel. On the mantle shelf stood a jar of long slender sticks about pencil thickness and of pitchy wood. These served as matches for grandfather's pipe, or for lighting candles.

In my boyhood days I used to watch, fascinated, the sparks that would ignite on the black charred fireplace wall when the coals were low. These sparks would not flame up, just creep through the gathered creosote — building fantastic shapes of floating clouds, birds, animals and finally, as if by magic, disappearing.

There really is magic in a fireplace.

Beautifying Your Cabin

Beautifying Your Cabin

Although I lay no claim to knowledge of Interior Decoration, there are a few essentials that I feel I dare suggest which can give to the inside of your cabin home the comfortable, simple, rugged beauty that will be in keeping with the structure and the setting.

I once saw a beautiful, truly pioneer, log cabin ruined by the lady of the house who transplanted the successful and lovely scheme of decoration for her city home to the primitive naturalness of the country. It did not fit.

A cabin of logs suggests its own motif in both line and color. We are getting away from the artificial. We are reviving the restful softness of woods coloring, the strength of straight lines and natural curves, with accents of brilliance for warmth on cold nights and light on cloudy days. To achieve this rather fierce charm of ruggedness blended with coziness has a fascination all its own. Your cabin can throw a spell over one in its rough welcome, gentled by the natural refinement of your personal

71

Door Latches and shutter catches

tastes and expressions. Even the flickering fireplace flames will enhance your cabin color scheme.

Cedar logs are tan in color with streaks of lighter tone all the way from light brown to cream. Cedar has a beautiful grain, so does hemlock when properly dressed down. Hemlock logs, however, when left to dry for a year tone down to a fine silvery gray. Cedar, thoroughly dry, may be dressed down with a draw shave reviving its natural color, and releasing that sweet pungent smell of the cedar woods. Dressed knotty white pine blends perfectly with a log cabin. You can use it for doors, window frames, cupboard and book shelves. It does not need a dark stain. Merely rub it down with boiled linseed oil, adding a coat of varnish. The knots will glisten, the lovely natural grain remains. Without this treatment white pine does not stay light but gets darker and darker as time goes on until it looks dark brown.

Don't miss the fun of having wrought iron hinges and latches. Plenty of imagination and personal symbolism can go into the choice of design for the door knocker to announce your visitors, the iron foot scraper, even the boot-jack, that are a part of your porch decoration, and too, door hinges, and pot-hooks. By now you must be saying, "I have no money to spend on wrought iron." You need not say it. Go to your hardware store or, better still to the general store in the country town. Ask for a pair of heavy barn hinges. You can get them from twenty-four to thirty inches long. Now hunt up the village blacksmith (or realize the fun of setting up a small forge of your own). Have the blacksmith reheat the metal, then pound it hard with a ball peen hammer, roughen it, with or without design, and it becomes wrought iron. From scraps of iron and with ingenuity, many delightful articles may be added to your cabin inside and out. Their rugged individuality suits your cabin motif. An old buggy wheel suspended from the rafters by log chains of iron may afford overhead lighting. Brackets for oil lamps add to their charm. Of course the tools for your fireplace and the pot-hooks become essentials.

Speaking of indoor fireplaces, I am tempted to say here: "Don't build this center of your home, your hearth, out of manufactured bricks if natural stone is anywhere available." Native stones belong to your setting; you can't improve upon them. Use them.

Your choice of flooring may be determined by your budget—or the availability of material. Flagstone if available. Hardwood (i.e. maple or oak) is preferable, but Georgia pine or fir, sanded, oiled and varnished do very well.

For old times' sake, and for easy cleaning and wear, remember to include rag rugs, the kind grandma used to make out of odds and ends of garments or old material. Here is a chance to learn the knack of hooking rugs. The homespun materials are in keeping with the

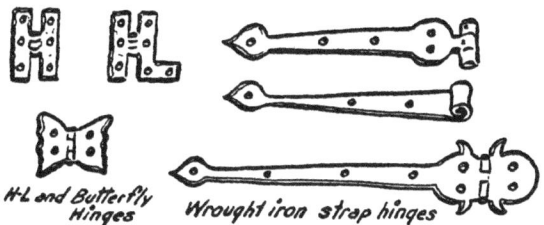

H, HL and Butterfly Hinges   Wrought iron strap hinges

73

early American designs. We found that burlap had that handmade look. Burlap can be purchased by the yard from your bag company. We used it for cabin drapes. It blended perfectly with the wood tones. To enliven it a bit we stenciled the borders with conventional figures in bright colors. In a cabin in the mountains, two friends of ours have created designs that express, totem pole fashion, the episodes, the fun that have grown into the life of the cabin. These designs are repeated on dishes, cushions, book ends even hammered into some of their iron and copper work.

One other element that adds to the welcome in your cabin is, in homely phrase, a sweet, clean smell. On this point there is need of precaution. A tightly closed, poorly ventilated cabin will soon grow musty and will disappoint you. In the gable ends, and very near the top, I have a small window swung on hinges. Attached to its top is a latch string long enough so that I may open and shut the twelve inch opening at will. The last thing I do, when leaving my cabin, is to open the ventilators. They are copper screened—and close under the roof ends so that neither snow nor rain drifts in. Whether you re-enter in a week or in a month you will find your cabin fresh and sweet with the fragrance of the pine or cedar logs.

One other precaution you must take to preserve this fresh clean smell: If you burn wood in a stove, you must guard against the drip of creosote from the stove pipe. Wood smoke builds up creosote in your chimney flue, and also in the stove pipes leading to it. When the stoves are idle, moisture gathers. Rain also may enter an uncapped chimney and carry the creosote along. It leaves a pungent and offensive odor.

I once had such a stove. The pipe ran straight up for five or six feet above the stove. Then came the elbow and and two lengths of pipe which ran horizontally into the main chimney. Snow drifted into the chimney and settled in the horizontal part of the pipe. On arrival we started our fire. The snow melted and drip, drip, drip, from the joints of the pine came the black, sticky, stinking creosote. It sputtered over the floor and even the side walls. Creosote is the worst stuff to scrub away, and the smell will not fade out.

I have since learned that I do not always need to pipe into a brick chimney. I run the stove pipe straight up and through a triple cylinder, metal smoke-stack right through the roof. It is perfectly safe—and cheaper than the brick. I also learned that when the pipe sections are fitted one into the other, it is wise to nest the top section into the one below. This does away with any possible leak of smoke or moisture. The creosote is also controlled.

WROUGHT IRON FOOT SCRAPERS

Solomon's
Seal

LANDSCAPING YOUR CABIN SETTING

A log cabin needs plenty of sunlight. Logs are a fine insulation against heat, but they do absorb moisture and need to dry out. A cabin buried among too many shade trees can be dark and damp on rainy days. Leave a bit of grass spot round the house. It really adds to the charm. One cabin builder whom I observed went to the other extreme. He decided on a two acre lawn. With bull dozers and other machinery, he levelled his grounds—tore out wild shrubs, bushes and small trees. He planted clover and grass. The results were beautiful but he spent much of each summer thereafter behind a lawn mower.

Salvage those small trees and bushes. Leave the natural setting, opening a vista here and there, a path or two; but let Nature, not the nursery, provide your setting. Chances are that you will add a lot of extra work and expense without improving things if you go for flower beds and lawns in a big way. A Cabin in the Woods should be so simple in its setup that after unlocking the door, opening the windows, bringing out a chair or two, you should be able to settle down and enjoy living. Breathe deep and relax.

If you want a rock garden, find it. There will be a spot somewhere that with a few touches of recognition and encouragement can become one. If you would like a lily pond, or even a fountain, seek your hillside spring. With

Blue Violet

a bit of piping you can guide the flow into a nearby saucer-like depression. Cover a space about ten feet wide and twelve long with cobble stones, a bit of sand and gravel. Transplant a few waterplants into the rock crevices. The fountain may be piped from below the stones. The overflow can be controlled and guided with a few clay tile. The cost need be little. These are playthings, not work. It is satisfying to create.

Always leave something for the next visit, the next summer. Outdoor living with its relaxing, creative activity will fulfill the true purpose, the dream that went into our Cabin Craft.

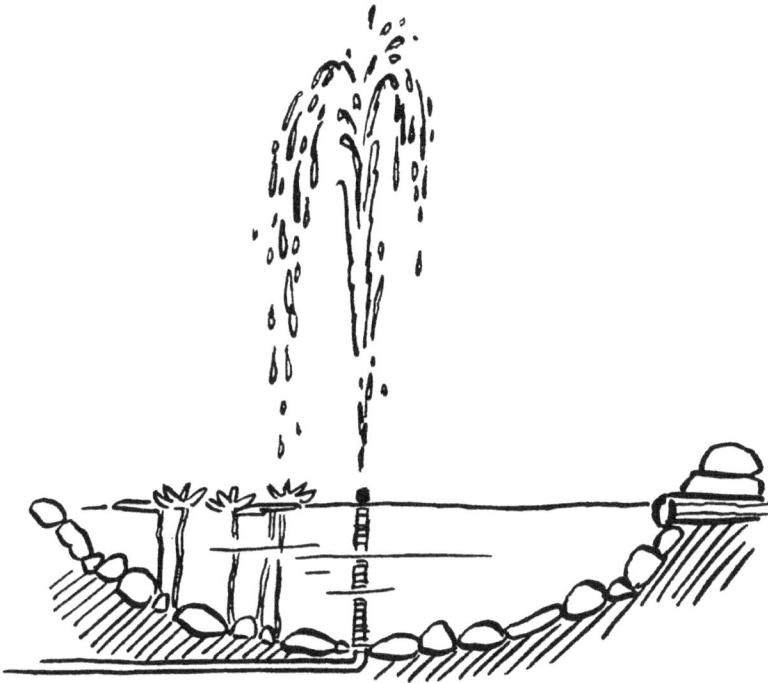

Liberty

Liberty

This hidden word has burned in the hearts of men since the beginning of time. This sacred word, after ages, was flowered in America. Our stubborn forebears argued, quarreled, fought and died for it. Liberty — that magic word that lured men from all corners of the earth to our shores — men who risked their all just to live for a short spell in the atmosphere of a free man. Liberty — that promised a man he could look his fellowmen in the face and not be cowed in their presence.

Men of the ages have longed and struggled for this great freedom — many have died without strength to find it. Others with great faith that "men were created equal" stood fast until, after many generations, America, the symbol of liberty, took shape. Finally it was ours — a society of people in good old Abe Lincoln's words, "By the people, for the people, of the people."

Liberty that leaves a man free to fight — yes, with the loaded shotgun on the mantle shelf — Indians — wild animals — or the thief in the night. Liberty that implies property and

wild
Mustard

Clover

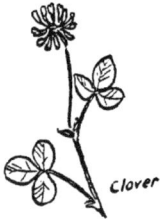

spiritual rights and the freedom to protect those rights.

Liberty presupposes my faith in the power of my vote. My vote means to me the influence of "We, the people." As Americans we do have faith in the power of our individual vote. That is most important.

When the "divine right of kings" held sway, kings enjoyed their sacred privilege by the faith and good will of the people. The "divine right of kings" actually came from the people. But most kings, like all other mortals, soon forgot the gift of the common people and too soon took for granted that they, and they alone, held the one and only key to heaven and that, therefore, they in turn carried authority directly from God. They then abused the authority. This abuse continued for centuries until the kingly world revolted and threw out most of their kings, trading them for democracies, dictatorships — anything but a king and oppression.

Contrast this to the American way of life. We do not belong to any king. Nor does any king hold sway over our right to heaven. In America the government belongs to "we, the people." The government belongs to me, the individual, and I belong to God. It is through my conscience, as a free man, that I account to my God for my conduct, my relations with my neighbor, and the way I vote. I am a free man under God.

Great Burdock

Yet I must have respect for the laws of my land — a law which will assure order. Too many of us become a law unto ourselves. If this became universal, God help us; we would have anarchy. Anarchy is a close cousin to lawlessness. This is no longer liberty. Even the traffic light on the corner is a symbol of the law. A free man obeys it.

I've heard many definitions of Democracy. Here is one of my own. I challenge you to write yours.

"I want to read what I please. I want to think what I please. I want to say what I please, provided I can respect my neighbor's property, his religion, his politics and his racial background. I want to pay my taxes gladly (even though I may grouch about the way the government spends it.)"

For this great freedom, I thank God. I can through my taxes pay and if need be, fight for those sacred privileges to be a free man, an American — long live LIBERTY!

Your Flag Pole

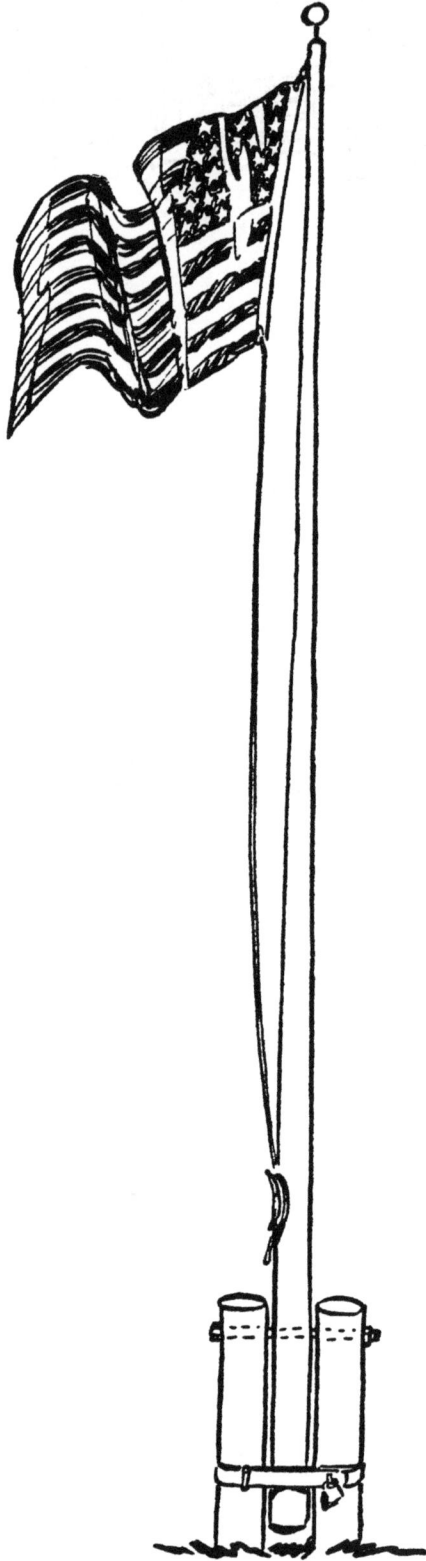

Your Flag Pole

No camp is complete without a flag and flag pole. We hoist the flag when we arrive. It says to our friends and neighbors, "We are in and you are welcome."

Were it not for the meaning woven through the years into this Flag of our Nation, we might not be enjoying the privilege of building and owning a cabin in the woods.

There are a few mechanical problems in erecting a flag pole. If you just dig a hole in the ground and drop the pole in, packing it with stones and dirt, be sure it does not lean a bit off center. This can be very distressing later! After setting it is hard to change. So, save yourself needless hard work and disappointment. Before packing the earth around the pole be sure it stands 100% perpendicular. Tie a pebble to a piece of string about two feet long. Stand about fifty feet away from the pole and hold up the string—the pebble at the bottom, of course. Here is a true vertical. Have your helpers move the pole right or left until it is in line with your plumb line. Circle the pole so that you have trued it from several angles. Now brace it securely. Only when you are satisfied that it is actually perpendicular, fill in around the base with dirt and stones. Tamp it in firmly. Keep it braced for a week until it settles.

I have taken for granted that before you raised the pole your pulley and halyard were in place. It is a wise man who whips the halyard lines or at least ties them together. I once had the embarrassment of having one of the lines slip out of my hand. In less time than it takes to tell it, the halyard had run out of the pulley forty feet above. Old Glory did not fly that day. It is not an easy matter to get up to the top of a graceful pole — even with a ladder. Since lines wear out or decay and have to be replaced, I now use a double post with the flag pole between — a three-quarter inch pivot or axle running between and through the two posts and the pole — about five feet above the ground. At the bottom of the pole place an iron band attached firmly around the two posts. Fasten with a large hasp and padlock. Your blacksmith will make this for you. By unlocking the hasp you can now lower the pole to the ground. It can be repaired, painted and set up again without risk to life and limb.

Use a bit of imagination in dressing up the flag pole's top. A weather vane, maybe, instead of the traditional ball. Many quaint and individual flag symbols may add to the fun and usefulness of your flag pole tradition.

A Dining
Room Suite

A Dining Room Suite

Here is an outdoor dining room outfit that costs little or nothing. On my own place I built the table on top of a small tree stump. I cut off the stump twenty-five inches above the ground —allowing for four inches of thickness of table top. If you have no convenient stump, dig a hole where you want your table. Use your post-hole digger for the neat hole—about thirty inches deep. Set in it a six inch log about five feet long. Stamp it in firmly. With your cross cut saw level off the top at the desired height.

If you have small soft wood trees or saplings four to six inches in diameter, cut these in four foot lengths, split them in half smoothing one side flat with your axe. Next, lay these logs flat side to the ground and anchor them together with two cleets. Now place them on your post flat side up. Put four angle braces beneath. Cover the top with linoleum and your table is ready for use.

Splitting saplings for table tops can best be done with iron wedges. Your extra axes can serve this purpose. Start at one end of the log by driving your axe slightly, but exactly in the center. Drive the second axe into the crack you have started—about twelve inches farther along. By the time the third axe is in place, the first axe will drop as the split log gives way. Of course if you have lumber, you can build a table top with much less effort!

Peg-leg stools are a practical and natural companion to a tree-top table. They are easy to make and will last a lifetime in the open. For four stools you will need two sixteen inch long logs about twelve inches in diameter. Split these in half, again smoothing the flat side with your axe. On the round under side bore three one and a half inch holes about three inches deep. These should be at an angle so that the legs will spread. Next cut twelve two inch thick branches, three for each stool. Taper each at one end to fit snugly into the bored holes. A three-legged stool fits more easily on uneven ground than one with four legs. With the help of a buddy your complete dining room set can be built in an hour or two.

Perhaps you may have no twelve inch soft wood on your place. If not, go to your nearest telephone or electric company. For a small fee

94

they will sell you used telephone poles. Often they have poles too short for their purposes but adequate for yours.

So, for this project you will need (1) a buddy to share the fun; (2) a post hole digger; (3) a cross cut saw; (4) an augur; (5) an axe; (6) carpentry tools; (7) wood from your woodlot. Lastly, energy and imagination if you don't want to sit on the ground.

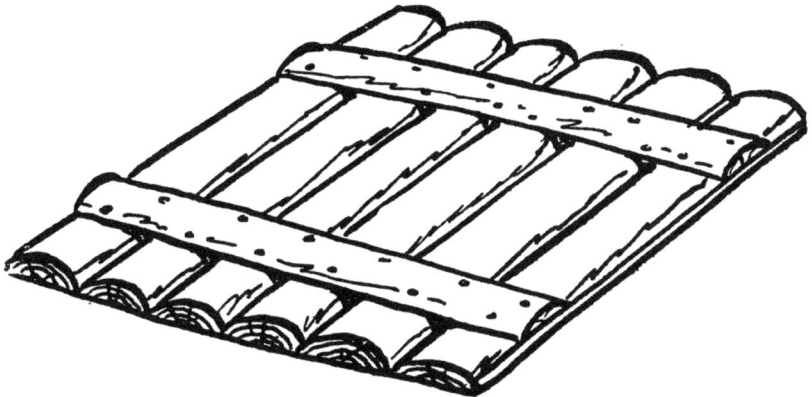

Cabin Tools

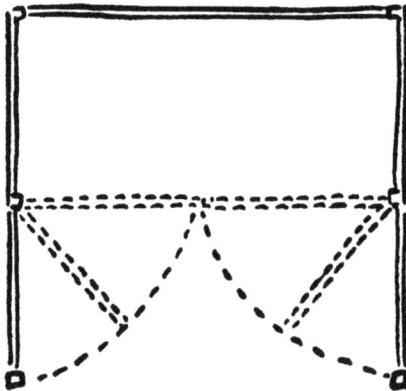

98

Cabin Tools

KEEP 'EM SHARP

There is nothing in my experience more trying, more time wasting and disheartening than to attempt to carve a turkey, repair a door, or build a cabin with dull or inadequate tools.

A tool chest and a workshop will always be a part of your Cabin Craft — so prepare for it. Stock the essential implements that you will need if you are to get the real satisfaction from your efforts. Good tools need protection — a roof — and a lock. If your building occurs on weekends and scattered days a small shed is a good investment. The shed may later serve for a chicken coop, storage or wood shed. A tent is probably sufficient coverage if you can stay on the job until it is complete.

Either build or buy a work-bench with a vise attached. You just must have the vise to grip firmly the boards upon which you want to work. Your tool chest should contain hammers, a level, screw drivers, square, chalk, a soft pencil or two, tough string for plumb lines and an

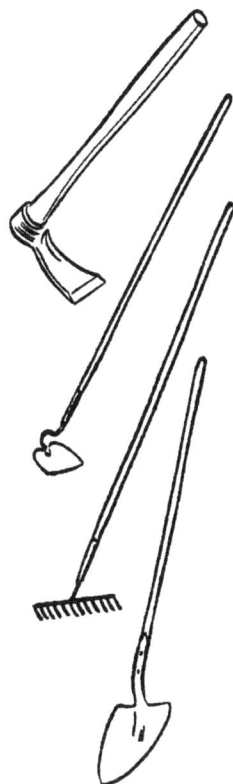

99

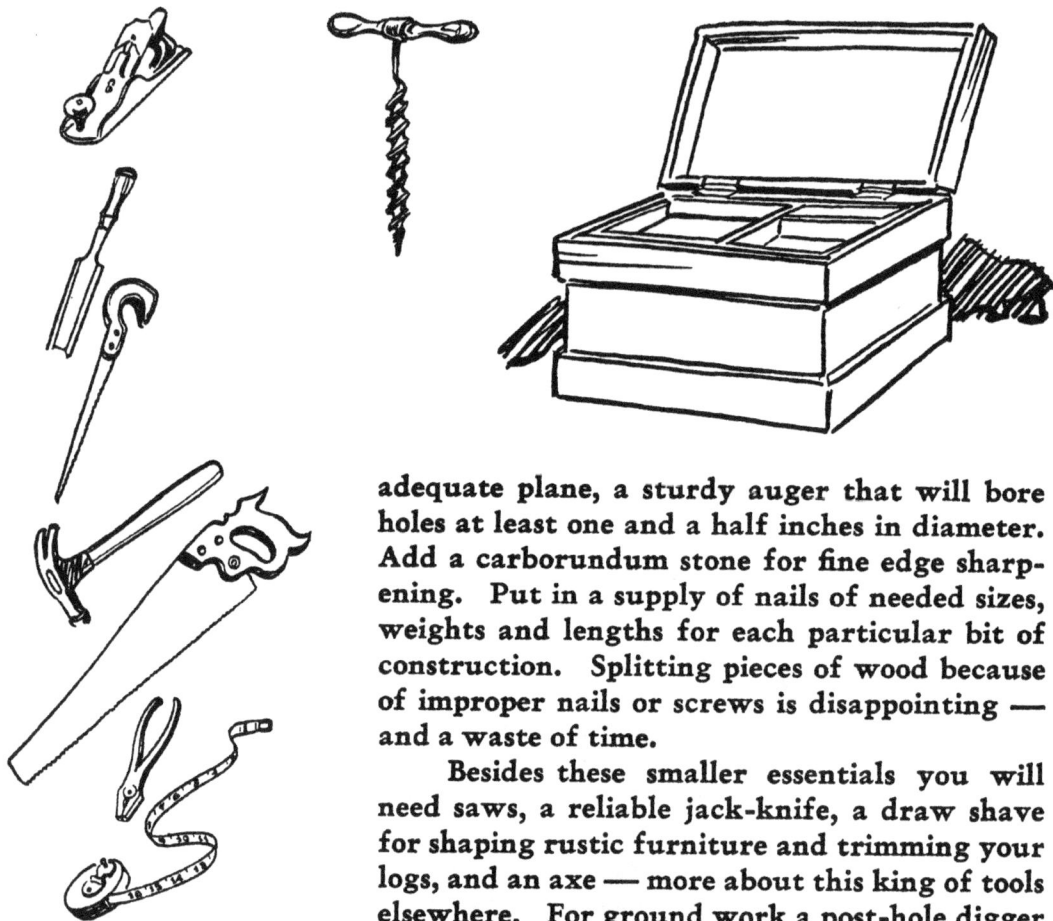

adequate plane, a sturdy auger that will bore holes at least one and a half inches in diameter. Add a carborundum stone for fine edge sharpening. Put in a supply of nails of needed sizes, weights and lengths for each particular bit of construction. Splitting pieces of wood because of improper nails or screws is disappointing — and a waste of time.

Besides these smaller essentials you will need saws, a reliable jack-knife, a draw shave for shaping rustic furniture and trimming your logs, and an axe — more about this king of tools elsewhere. For ground work a post-hole digger is a great time saver. A pickaxe, a crow bar, the shovels, rake and hoe, a grub axe.

Now something to keep the tools sharp. An old-fashioned grindstone goes well with your cabin craft. On a rainy day I get the grindstone working and sharpen up my axes. This done, I get my collection of jack-knives,

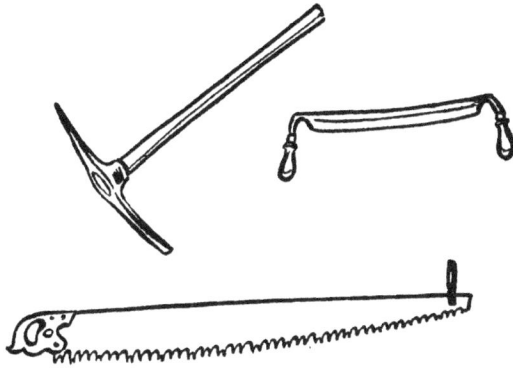

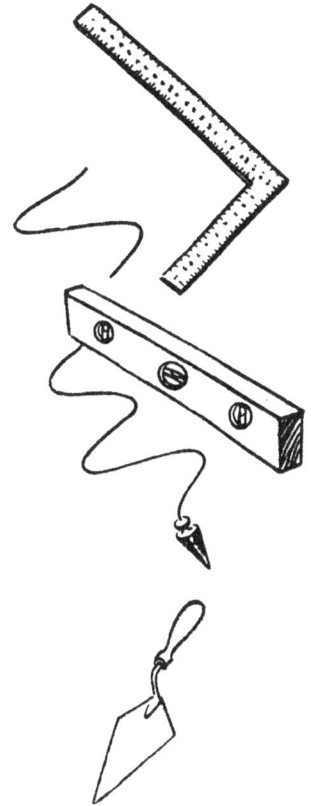

bowie knives — and just to keep in right with the kitchen folk, the butcher knives and kitchen knives. There is nothing like a grindstone for really sharpening steel. The water dripping from the can above prevents overheating of the metal. I'm sure you will now defend the emery or carborundum wheel. I have one connected with power. It is good for rough work, but too often I have burned a good piece of steel by overheating. Once burned, the life is gone from the steel. To properly grind an axe or knife takes practice — a steady hand and patience. Edge tools should be held against the stone at an angle so that the sharpest part of the edge barely touches the stone. As you wear the rough high spots down toward the fine edge, your blade will even up.

The flat fine carborundum stone is most valuable for the final finishing. To give your tool its final keen edge use an eight inch flat carborundum stone.

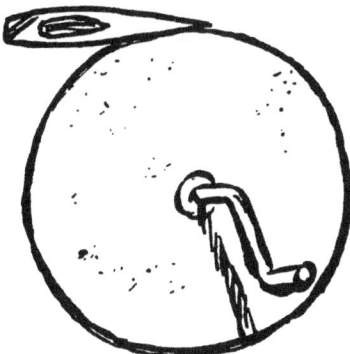

THE AXE

Now if you are a white collared city "guy" who goes to the woods for weekends, who has most of his work done for him, you won't need an axe. For the real cabin builder the axe is his best friend. With an axe you can fashion a rough cabin or hunting shelter; with an axe you can build traps and snares to catch wild animals for food; with an axe you can blaze your way through dense woods — notching a return trail; with an axe you can cut firewood for cooking and for warmth. Without an axe I should feel helpless in the woods. It is the first "must" on my list of tools.

At this point, if you are a novice in axemanship, you might expect further instruction on "How to handle an axe." Any expert would agree with me that such written directions would be bad teaching. Here is a craft that can not be gained from books. The skill must be handed down by one who knows — it must be learned in the doing.

Many books have been written on how to play golf. They may serve for winter sport beside a fireplace. But to benefit from real instruction the amateur still goes to the golf course — asks the guidance of a golf "pro." The "pro" knows the why and how of grips, stance, position and he teaches right out on the course. So in learning the use of an axe. Find the farmer who cuts his own wood from his woodlot or the lumber-jack or craftsman who

earns his salt with an axe. Either one will say,
"Well, come along to the woodpile — we'll cut
firewood while we are learning." This will result in added skill for you — and more wood for
the woodpile — and you won't have to pay five
dollars an hour for this most practical instruction.

As your skill improves you will not be satisfied with one axe. I have seventeen in actual
use. A bit of a hobby? Yes — but each axe has
a special purpose. They differ in shape, weight
and length. They range from the dainty light
axe for fine work to the broad axe used in
pioneer days for squaring logs to build beams
and block houses. The broad axe is little used
today but I wouldn't part with mine.

Some axes are for cutting, others for splitting. Cutting axes must be sharp to be effective.

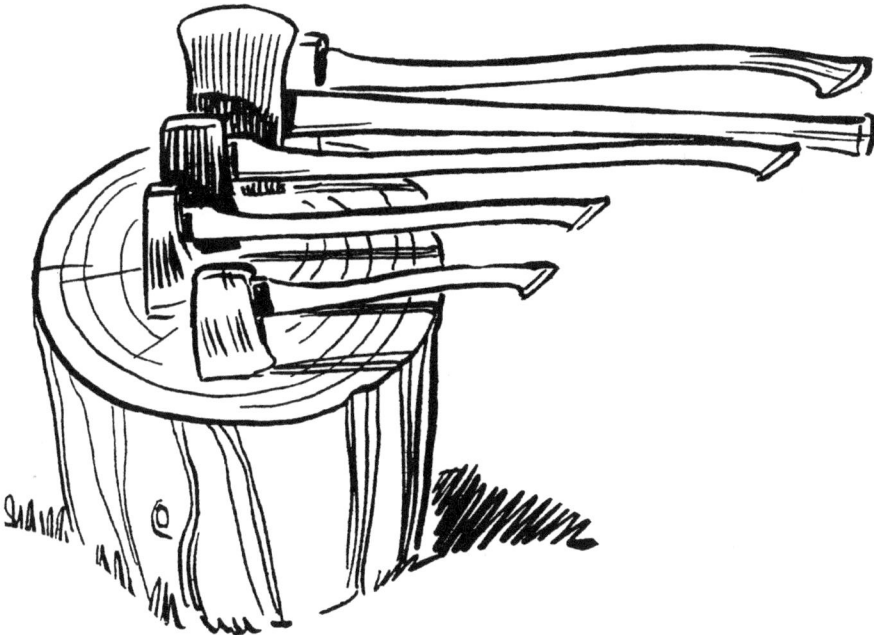

Keep them sharp — razor sharp and you will respect them. I once saw a lumber-jack in Northern Wisconsin shave his partner with a two-bitted axe — not for the sake of the shave but to demonstrate what he meant by a razor sharp edge on his axe.

An old tree stump provides a center for sport and healthy exercise for my guests when we play Indian and throw the hatchet. I have four old axes for this purpose. The object of the game is to throw the hatchet 20 or 30 feet so that it will stick into the old stump. It's not at all difficult. Throw the axe overhead with the blade pointing forward. The axe must make a complete revolution before it hits the stump. So if you miss, stand a little farther back. Vary your position until you connect. Each axe and each contestant's force varies.

No camp is complete without one or more axes.

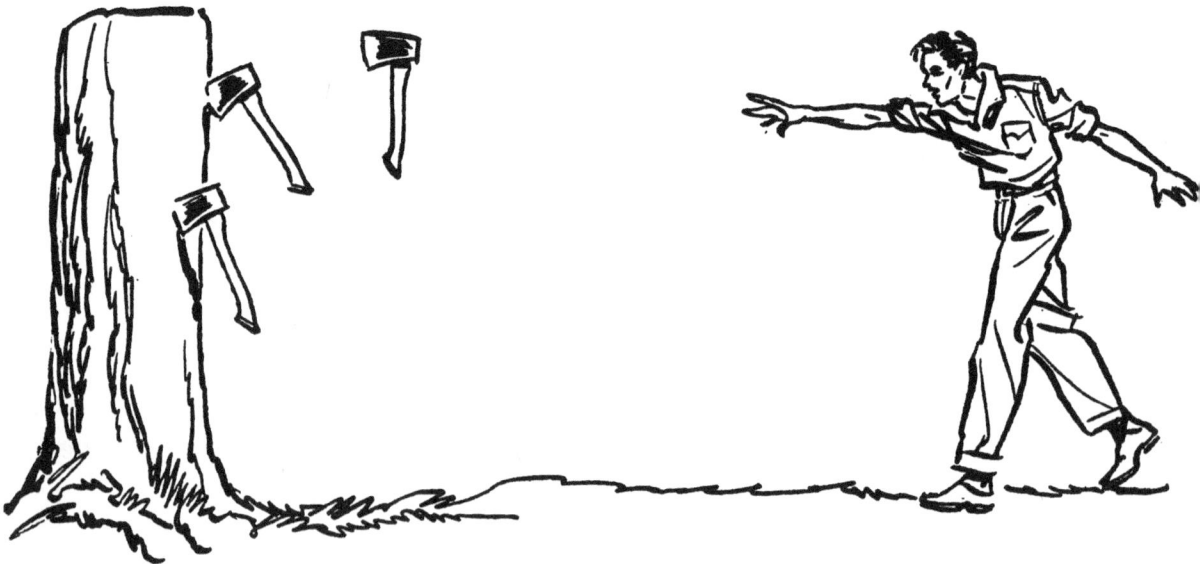

KNIVES

Next to the axe in usefulness is the woods-man's knife. In this day and age we are inclined to think of the pocket knife as a dainty pearl handled affair for sharpening pencils and cutting string on packages. No true woodsman would tolerate such a tool.

Knife collecting, I must confess, is quite as much a hobby of mine as my hoarding of axes. A few of them are rare antiques. The case of one is made from a deer's foot — hair and all. Another, it is claimed, saved the life of my grandfather when faced with a bear. Caught without a gun grandfather fought it out with his knife. Scared and bruised, his life was saved by the knife.

A woodsman and cabin builder needs both a jack-knife in his pocket and a stout bowie knife in a sheath attached to his belt. Hunters too need this sharp bowie knife, for a deer, after being shot, should at once be bled and dressed.

In my collection are knives from three to eighteen inches in length. I have a set of fine carving tools, each of them razor sharp. It is fun to show your skill with a roast of beef or a well browned fowl. If your knife is sharp the carving is quite simple—just steady the roast with a large fork and draw your knife back and forth. With a little practice you can cut roast beef in even thick or paper-thin slices. For fowl I prefer a short thin blade. It is easier to find and separate the joints. A longer thin blade should be at hand for carving the slices of white breast-meat.

In our family—as in most families—are swords from past wars. We had several: commanders' swords three feet long, bayonets, a fencing saber, a dirk and short dagger for close-in engagements. These tools were designed for killing men. They are refashioned now into implements for peacetime pursuits—for carving and for pruning.

The commander's sword was a piece of excellent steel. Using my emery wheel and grindstone I cut it in two, regrinding the blades into fine carving knives that are among my prize cutting tools.

Good steel is sometimes hard to get. If you are one of those who must have a really good knife of the best tempered steel—and are willing to do the necessary grinding, reconvert an old steel file. Steel files must be made of the best tempered steel. They can be ground to the shape and size desired. A twelve inch file can be ground into a perfect carving knife.

The story is told of two ancient kings who demonstrated to each other their skill with the sword. The first king, a giant in size, drew forth his heavy powerful weapon. With one mighty blow he severed an iron bar one inch thick. The second king drew forth his slender, delicate, razor sharp blade. He drew it across a feather pillow—splitting the case with such hair-precision no bit of down was spilled. The moral to this bedtime story is not important here. For me, I prefer the delicate skill that comes from sharp well-balanced tools, handled by men who appreciate how to use them.

NAILS

To choose the right kind and size of nails to be driven into wood is as important as knowing what ingredients go into a cake, or which golf club to use for making a particular shot. The purpose of the nail is to hold two pieces of wood together. If the pieces of wood are thick, i.e. nailing two pieces of two by fours together, then longer and stouter nails are required. If to nail two one-inch boards together, then a smaller nail will do.

There are cut nails, common wire nails, horseshoe nails, finishing nails, penny nails and others. For our purpose in the use of nails which will deal mostly with joinery and carpentry, there are three kinds of nails to be considered. They are called "penny" nails, "box" nails and "finishing" nails.

Penny nails run from two-penny to sixty-penny nails. A two-penny is one inch in length, a three-penny one and one-quarter inches long and so on up to sixty-penny which is about seven inches in length.

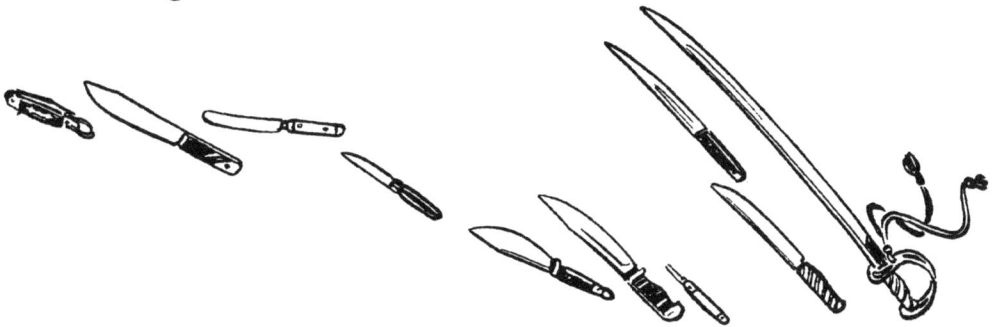

The penny nail is a heavy nail with a sturdy shank that can be driven hard with a heavy hammer without bending. Never choose a nail longer than the thickness of the wood you want to nail together. If you choose a nail longer so that it sticks out on the other side, you are wasting that piece of the nail; but more than this, you add nothing to the holding strength of the nail. It should be thoroughly buried into the two pieces of wood you are binding together. To turn over the piece of protruding nail indeed locks the nail into the wood, but in so doing there is danger of partly driving it back and your boards are not tight fitting.

Box nails run about the same size as penny nails, but are thinner and for finer work.

Lastly, finishing nails are for cabinet work. These have small heads which when driven into the wood can be sunk deeper with a nail-set so that no part of the nail is above the surface of the wood.

With the last stroke of the hammer which finally plants the nail in your board, care must be taken to hit gently so as not to injure the grain of the wood, if you want to produce fine workmanship.

Why All This Hard Work?

V. Aures

Why All This Hard Work?

I'm writing this article in the heart of the Connecticut hills. I courted my one and best girl here thirty years ago; so loving thoughts again start into being. The rugged, rocky countryside has a deeper meaning. I understand today, as I did not in those young days, how important a part rock, hill and forest played in helping our pioneer forefathers to grow strong, sturdy and stable.

I gaze from a high vantage point, down upon a rollicking brook that is finally arrested by a stone wall and dam. Once the power here developed served a grist mill to which farmers brought their grain and corn for grinding. It is idle now, yet still a symbol of pioneer resourcefulness and cooperation. The murmuring, gurgling stream still fills its eternal purpose as it sloshes, splashes, dashes from mill dam to mill dam, on and on to the endless sea.

Below the mill pond are garden plots boxed in by huge stone walls — walls built by determined settlers over two centuries ago. They represent the toil and trials of simple earnest folk. The stones were heavy and hard

to pry loose from the earth, hard to move great distances. Help was scarce. Oxen hitched to stone boats were slow. And yet these walls, enclosing many a half-acre, have stood these hundred or two hundred years — erect, intact, still paying tribute to early American builders. They tell, also, of the endless effort it took to clear the land that food might be raised for family and occasional friend. Boulders, rocks and more rocks which had lain undisturbed since the glacial days, gave way to the strength and determination of these early Americans. In turn, they gave these qualities to America.

The labor was toil of devotion and high courage. It was given willingly to fight the elements, wild animals, unfriendly Indians — to wrest security and a home from the native soil. It bespeaks love of home with all its love-giving implications. Here were men unafraid of hard work. They called it not toil. To them it was life and liberty — their path to happiness, security, and God.

You must recognize by now that I, too, was reared in this hard school of trial and toil. I am glad for the lessons it taught me. I am sorry for the lads of today who are born with a "silver spoon" and who never have the opportunity to face life's realities or learn the relationship between work and reward, — responsibility and privilege: I like "Teddy" Roosevelt's thinking when he said, "When you play, play hard. When you work, don't play at all."

One of the rich stories in my neighbor's family is built around his Great-grandfather Hiram back in 1830, when he built his own log cabin on rocky land for his wife Hannah. It was fourteen miles from the grist mill. After the first harvest he started off at dawn one morning with a sixty-pound sack of grain on his back. No ox cart or horse. He went on foot to the grist mill where with waterpower the grain was ground into flour. At the small general store he bought five cents worth of chocolate drops for his girl, gathered the latest gossip — the doings of President Jackson down in Washington — then carried his sack of flour fourteen miles home. The tallow candle was in the window. Hannah was sitting up to wait for him. He dropped the sack on the kitchen table and said, "Well, Hannah, I guess we won't starve for a while." What a man! With but sixty pounds of flour he yet knew that he could produce three square meals a day until his next trip to the mill and store. What a woman, to cast her lot with such a life! Their faith in each other and in the strength God gave them — faith that he could find wild roots, bear meat and grease with his trusted gun — faith in his axe with which he cut wood for winter warmth — faith in the recurrent spring, new plantings in an ever-widening garden as better tools, a mule or an ox made possible the removal of stumps and rocks. And so with only sixty pounds of the "bread of life," with Hannah's skill and their combined resourcefulness they

could make home secure, sweet and satisfying. I'm sure he took her close in his arms — and they went to bed and slept peacefully, dreaming sweet dreams. They, too, were building America. Uncle Dan Beard once said, "Those were the days when divorces were unpopular." Men stood by their women and women backed up their men for mutual security. They just did not walk out on each other because of silly frustrations. Their purpose was larger, deeper than this. They were home builders for America.

But I have wandered back through the years. Right here before me still stands the old mill — now silent. Near it since American Revolutionary days stands the Silver Mine Tavern. I talked with its present owner, John Byard, who knows and respects the history of the place. From him I heard how Sam Ryder, the venerable owner of the old mill, had maintained to the end that nothing could grind grain or turn a lathe like a river, and how, long after the mill had ceased to yield him a competence, he had lived on alone among the outmoded tools, the machinery of waterpower-days, dreaming always of rebuilding the dam. It was rebuilt. Water again filled the pond, but not until the property had passed into other hands. It is now a shrine to Yankee courage and enterprise.

Across the road from the Tavern stands the old Country Store. It is now filled with interesting antiques; but not so long ago it

housed the pot-bellied stove about which neighbors gathered to cuss and discuss the crops, the weather, the local politics. You can still see the tables, the old checker-boards where customers tried their skill while the storekeeper computed the value of the butter, eggs and potatoes in terms of yard goods or delicacies on his shelves.

The story is told of a women's temperance union which met on winter evenings in a room over the store, to ponder the evils of drink, undaunted by the disrespectful and raucous homage paid to their concerns by the menfolk at the public bar across the way.

Just half a mile up the Silver Mine River stands a famous saw mill still operated by waterpower. It has belonged to the Buttery family nearly one hundred years. Mr. Fred Buttery said, "This old mill was started in 1712. It's had the same dam, same machinery for over a hundred years. The wheels that gear into each other are still made of wood." He is a kindly old gentleman, unhurried, with steady eye and honest face that says, "I've earned my way by honest work." He'd still a bit of sawdust on his hat and shoulders. He, like Sam Ryder, swears "There isn't anything that can beat waterpower." A grand old gentleman still portraying the indomitable Yankee independence — the courage — the hard work that helped to build America.

What a rich heritage has been left us by these great and simple folk! Not only fabulous wealth for a great nation which their wildest imagination could not possibly have conceived, but a faith in the good earth — a courage and will to toil — a determination to fight and win and build anew, an American way of life and thought. We, today, you and I, must hold on to this same simple philosophy, must carry it on to keep America steady, to keep her great. It's worth all the hard work.

Weather Wise

Weather Wise

"It's going to rain," says my farmer friend. My own mind at this point reverts to the upper left-hand corner of the newspaper, or to the on-the-hour broadcast of weather reports. These weather observers do our thinking and interpreting for us. Thanks — but it is not enough. We have grown dependent on clocks, bells, whistles — mechanical devices. We have lost the ability to read the skies and the earth. Nature has always been full of advance information, would we but heed it. The city has dulled our perceptions. We idle at street crossings until a dummy green light flashes "safe crossing." A noon siren tells us it is time for lunch. We have forgotten to note the sun at the zenith. We no longer wait for that nice empty feeling in the pit of our stomachs. School bells regulate our children's lives. Time clocks and office hours or bus schedules determine for us a good day's work. What automatons we have permitted ourselves to become!

"It's going to rain!" Of course. But you can't see this from your office chair. I hope you need not always feel tied to factory or of-

fice, because if so your outdoor mind will grow dull. Soon birds, wild animals, trees and the skies which dome over you will lose their meaning. Let us heed the call of the outdoors before we become hot-house plants and have to say, "I can't take it."

The grandest life in the world, Brother, is in the out-of-doors — nature in the rough — elemental life — where storms play symphonies that interweave themes from the gurgling brooks and rushing creeks, varied by staccato sleet and rain increased into demoniac splendor of the wind; returning to the reposeful triumph as the sun bursts through the clouds. Storm or sunshine, it's God's weather and all weather is good.

When you build a roof over your cabin in the woods for warmth and security, and stay within that cabin, you shut out the sky. Instead, think of your living room as outdoors.

My friend John A. Stiles wrote, "There is no such thing as bad weather, only improper clothing. Who cares whether it is raining or not, as long as he is prepared for it? Have you ever asked yourself if you like rain? I love to stride along with the rain beating in my face. How wonderful to come home with your feet going squash, squash in your boots — then to take a hot bath, a rub down and sit before the fire reading a book, your body all aglow with the exercise, the bath and the increased circulation." How grand to have a friend to share enthusiasm. I, too, like to hike through a storm,

tucked into a long raincoat. Try spending half an hour sitting on a log watching the animal life before or after a storm. Stormy weather will bring you closer together. "Squirrel and I" seem to be buddies drawn closer through delight, perhaps fear of the storm. We like the fierce wild weather.

But let's get back to weather signs. "It's going to rain." How do we know? First, a shift of the wind. The lowering the cloud-ceiling announced by the swallows circling low. Grey nimbus clouds gather. Thunderheads pile up on the horizon. The robins' rain song. The small animals scurry for shelter. The herd of cattle huddle together. You, with eyes to see and wit to interpret, need no barometer to forecast a storm. There are signs, too, for the weather-wise that guide spring planting, that warn of a long hard winter. "Deep snow this year," says the farmer; "heavy lush foliage and the bees are hiving high. Bees always store honey high in the trees when snowbanks will be high." So, when you see them making a beeline for the tree-tops, mark it down there will be heavy snow that winter. "Early winter," says Leo, "rabbits already have their winter fur. Bird migrations are two weeks ahead of last year. Scarcely a berry or nut left to pick up. The creatures are taking no chances."

When you live with the weather, when your livelihood depends upon your awareness, you learn to watch the trembling of the aspens, the turning to the rain of willow and poplar

leaves. You pay attention to all the simple signs of changing weather — even the sweat on your water bucket — the sounds — the silences.

Fruit trees bud by the first warmth of spring sun. Sometime to an early, false warmth in April. Fruit growers fight to keep their orchards warm for just those few frosty nights. They build smudge fires. They cover their trees with canvas and build fires around among the trees. Sometimes they succeed. Sometimes not. Only the oak can be counted on as a weather prophet. In Wisconsin we planted corn when the oak leaves were the size of squirrels' ears. The oak will not respond to warm weather until it has really come and frosty weather is really gone. Grandma King said, "Never plant cucumbers (in New York State) until June 13th. If you do they will be scrawny."

So here you have an introduction to signs and "weather signals." An odd mixture of fact and "Old Wives' tales"—from rings around the moon to Grandpa's "rhumatiz" or aching corns. It is fun to cultivate the skill to be able to stick your finger dramatically into your mouth, then up above your head and announce with accuracy, "The wind is from the north" as you feel the sharp line of coolness on that side of your finger. We really need this trick when sailing in a small craft.

Queer how we humans think we can command nature. We build cities along the river banks and spend millions of dollars to build levees and dykes to keep out high water. Engineers think they have control, but each year, somewhere, the floods break through, inundating houses, farms, villages and bridges. Nature shows her power.

This I know: God has an ordered universe. The answers are there to be read. To understand nature is a step toward understanding God. The good green earth belongs to Him. He made the weather signs.

When The Snow
Is Deep

When The Snow Is Deep

It is winter-time. The snow is deep. Cold frosty night settles. Snow begins to drift. Then from earth and heaven a billowing storm of crystal flakes bites your face. Toes tingle and legs twinge with the in and out pull against the drifts. Time for snow-shoes and skis. Cover your ears. Pull up your collar. Tuck your chin into your muffler and keep going. A good steady gait will stir the blood and warm you as you carry your pack on your back.

Just where are we going on this bleak frosty, stormy night? We have left the city far behind. The car is parked on top of the hill in the barn of a neighborly farmer. We (my wife and I) hear a call from the wild as we trudge to our cabin. Is it a dog, a coyote, a wolf? The dark shadow of our cabin looms through the storm — black, cold, forbidding. The trick latch quickly opens the door. Tinder and kindling prepared on the last trip, lie ready for the match. Shadows yield to the glowing, sparkling fire in stove and fireplace. Cold changes to warmth and we peel off our snowy outer garments. Within the hour our cabin

127

will be ready to reward our four expected guests with its warm radiance, fragrant with steaming coffee.

They come. Each laden with packsacks of duffel, woolens, food and fixings for the week-end. (No going back to the grocery store for added supplies.) Such an adventure calls for careful planning. On snow-shoes or skis they trudge breathlessly up the last slope. I go out to meet them, as I hear their merry shouts and laughter, and help to pull the toboggan, now laden with duffel. Tomorrow it will be ready to give fun and excitement. Packs are lowered onto the piles of cord wood sheltered on the porch. We stomp our feet and pant our greetings — breathing deep. The kitchen broom comes into play as we sweep each other free of clinging snow. Finally all are inside, toasting "fore and aft" before the blazing warmth. We need to dry out a bit.

Do you, now, my reader, feel "goose pimples" and shiver at the thought of sleeping in a cabin on a zero night? Read on a bit. You are missing one of the grandest of winter adventures, a winter week-end in the woods.

If you have sleeping bags or plenty of blankets (four woolen ones are essential) you can nestle in and let the fires go out. If you have less, one of the party must be the watch-

man and rebuild the fires every three hours. Either way, you will sleep well and dream sweet winter dreams. I keep a half dozen quilts in the cabin for those guests who may be inexperienced and so are "caught a bit short."

Clothes for the winter fun should include two pairs of woolen socks, good shoes, an extra pair if you have no overshoes. (I prefer galoshes). A woolen shirt, a sweat shirt and of course warm underwear. Better get out grandfather's red woolen undershirt and drawers. No wonder our pioneer fathers "could take it" in the woods — good or bad weather. They were prepared to take nature in their stride. So can we.

The group relaxes. Oh, boy! in for the week-end! No cares. No worries. No jangling telephones. The wind howls increasingly; packs the tiniest cracks with insulation of snow that makes the cabin even more secure. Supper is underway. Two kettles of steaming vegetables; fireplace biscuits in the reflector oven. The aroma taxes our patience. But wait no longer. A bowl of savory soup is served to each as we sit about watching the fire flames and the last act . . . the smoking grill. The coals leap into momentary flame as the rich steak-grease drips. "Ready with the rare steaks," and the discriminating are fed. A moment more

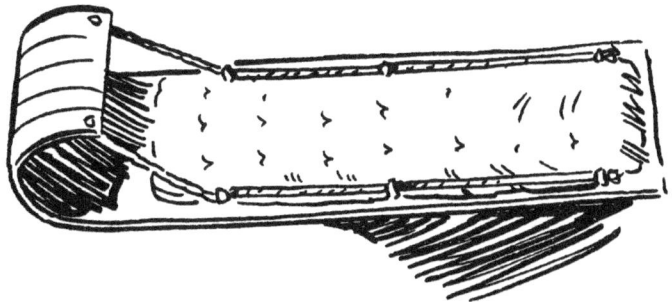

and even the chef admits that the dinner is a feast for kings.

Cooking over a glowing open fire can be done with a nicety, and to the entertainment of the guests. Sly remarks will be passed. Interesting queries, too, from the housewife who knows only the kitchen stove, wood, gas or electric technique. Fireplace cooking requires a bit of different skill. Onions and potatoes, in their "jackets" are dropped deep into the fireplace and covered with four inches of coals. Leave them for an hour. Dig them out, brush off the ash. You never tasted the like.

The fire dies down a bit. The candles on the table flicker softly. Deep contented sighs and easy conversation rise with the pipe and cigarette smoke. Someone draws the last delicious drops from the copper coffee kettle. The movement breaks the spell and the group is in action once again. All the lamps are lighted. The kitchen crew clear up, for we've found that half the fun comes from sharing all of the living in a cabin in the woods. The smouldering logs are set ablazing with a small piece of wood or two. Wood for the night, kindling for the morning are brought in. Beds made

snug and tight to climb into. Food is prepared against spoiling or freezing. The icebox will keep the cold out in winter, if temperature is zero. An added hot brick will keep it warm. We are ready for the evening fun.

Out comes the box of games — Bridge? Anagrams for the wordsters? Jigsaws? Monopoly? Sometimes we just yarn, cracking hickory and walnuts gathered in the fall. Sometimes we vie at toasting marshmallows or try our skill at candle dipping. Whatever the beginning of a winter evening, the end is always the same — the magic of the quiet — of the leaping flames — inspiring security, and our deeper thoughts well up in that last half-hour before going to bed. The chill of night is held back by the gleam of fire on the hearth. The curling flames and smoke are in control. When February winds are most persistent at the windows, when drifting snow gathers at the corner of each pane, our fireplace is a glowing, yes, a living symbol of the warmth and security of home and family and friends. It warms the feet, hands and body, but it also warms the heart. The slow steady glow of the backlog, the spit and sparkle of the deep lingering coals stir warm companionship,

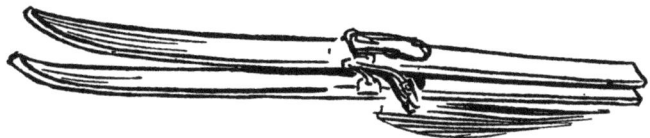

invite imagination, philosophies, close confidence. On such a night one of our guests* wrote by candlelight in the cabin loft, these lovely lines which expressed so perfectly our mood —

Blow out the lamp —
The candles and the hearth
Will light forever our encircled thoughts.

Outside spreads wide the meditative night.
Snow on the hills, the lake composed by cold,
This crouching roof, frost-fanged, drips by the
    chimney place,
Breaking the stillness where its heart is warm.

Sweet friends, beloved voices, deathless
    thoughts,
Holding man's balance in a reeling world;
High thoughts, as ageless as this flame on stone.

Timeless as water from the underground,
Pervasive and essential as the air.
Utterly indestructible they are.

They are the tools that never shall show rust;
The Prophet used them when he wrought with
    men:
We share their use, and will them when we pass
To our unspent, incalculable seed.

*Mary Boynton Parke.

The Barn Dance

The Barn Dance

Dancing in the early days was done not only by the young folks, but by father, mother, aunt and uncle—and occasionally even grandpa took a whirl just to prove he was quite a "buck" in his day. The barn dance was a family—yes, a neighborhood affair. Today we have turned this delightful and rhythmic art over to the youngsters and let them find their "canned music" through "Juke boxes." — Worse still, in taverns without any of the atmosphere of the community spirit and neighborliness.

It just wasn't a barn dance without everybody present. The night before, the young folks came over to sweep the barn floor clean of hay. I think the best barn dance of the year was the one in late September. It was the harvest dance. Haymows were bulging. Corn shocks were stacked artistically about the edges of the barn floor. Orange colored pumpkins added brightness. We didn't need to buy decorations. We had them on the land for the taking. There is something most unusual in the delightful smell of the hay mow.

The neighbors gathered from miles around sometimes like this for a "raisin'," sometimes for threshing and corn husking and sometimes on a Sunday just for the fun of getting together. Babies were parked on the double beds in the house and were peeked at or tended to by their fond mothers. Farmer fiddlers did double duty playing and calling or partnering their girls. "Bill, meet my Betty." "Jim, Sue's my girl. Now you keep clear." Jim, the pioneer version of Beau Brummel, was a bit too easy with the women. The occasional resultant fist fight merely added zest to this crowd who knew life for what it was and who stuck by their code of fair play—loving 'til death. They accepted, too, an occasional fall from grace. There was a "shot gun marriage." The sons have come through and have made their places among the solid citizens.

There were girl friends, raucous laughter, rough jokes, shy flirtations, but true to nature, simple, when a boy thought he had found his best girl and shyly told her so as they sat on the old rail fence; barn dances that lasted 'til four in the morning—"swing your ladies, grand right and left, choose your partners"—more rhythm, laughter and heart-throbs than "soup to nut dinners and cocktails" can stir in us today.

Cider played its part, too. Some imbibed, others tasted, a few had signed the pledge. It was considered manly for men to hold their

136

"likker" and so some drank beyond their appetite and capacity. It wasn't held against them if they "larned their lessen."

And the buggy ride home with your best girl. That pet horse still holds aces over a "flivver." Just wrap the reins around the buggy whip in its socket, leave him to his own devices and he'd get you home, after stopping part way to deliver Betty. A horse is really man's best friend and he won't tell. Four-thirty a. m. — an hour to sleep — then milking to be done. Cows waiting after the long night's rest, udders filled with rich milk, needed milking at daylight; also silage and clean stalls. One didn't sleep until noon the next day. Living creatures who served you needed your care. Each day's work had to be done. Quite likely we all went to bed right after supper the next day to make up for our reckless frivolity the night before.

Somehow in these modern years we "oldsters" have watched our younger generation bring in the modern Tango, Foxtrot to the blair and blast of pounding, thumping music until we have let the lead of the family dancing parties give way to the younger set — and looked upon ourselves as old fashioned. Indeed, let them be modern. They will anyway; but let us not forget the values that came out of the community barn dance for both young and old. We still all of us need to grow and to dance and to play together.

Thrift

Thrift

Thrift is a habit. It has a purpose. It's that stable quality which makes a man say "I've had enough." Thrift runs deeper than saving money. It is also conserving health, avoiding nervous tension, useless arguments. Thrift frowns on wasted time and things. Being niggardly is not being thrifty, for thrift invites generosity within reason. "To earn a little and to spend a little less"; but in the spending, to spend wisely. To be provident; that, is, careful for the future. It reflects industry, frugality.

Grandma's thrift, when she suggested to us children to eat first the spotted apples from the barrel, resulted in our eating rotten apples all winter.

Well, enough of this! Our pioneers got on. My great-grandfather — yes, grandfather would turn over in his grave were he here to see the weekly demand by our children for one, two and three movies per week; toys by the dozen, and costly ones, purchased to give the kiddies happiness. You can't *buy* all the happi-

141

ness for humans. It must come from something deeper and from within. I still love a hand-made gift, a monogrammed handkerchief, a cedar-chest, a necktie rack. These are the "loving thoughts with a meaning."

If we are to survive as individuals, families, or as a nation, we need first to practice thrift as individuals and families so our national wealth and resources will continue to grow. "Uncle Sam" needs our moral, thrifty backing first. Most of all, sound home financing is the first guarantee of national financial security.

Sugarin'

Sugarin'

If your cabin is really in the woods and if you really live life in it, the urge of early spring, late February, early March will stir us to action out-of-doors. If further, it is located in the north country where sugar maples grow, you'll know that the sap is running. When days are warm and sunny; when nights are still frosty and clear — sap wells up from the good earth. Man may tap the abundance, extract sweetness, health and wealth from God-given nature. There never was a more delicate sugar flavor than maple syrup and maple sugar boiled down from the sap of the sugar-maple tree.

A healthy tree, in a normal sap season, produces twenty-four to thirty gallons of sap. Boiled down, this will produce nearly a gallon of rich maple syrup. Have you one tree, or a grove of them? With a bit of effort you can "sugar off." Just an iron kettle on the kitchen stove will do.

Bore a three-eighths inch hole in the tree about three feet from the ground. Bore it about two inches deep, pointing your brace and bit straight in. Next drive in tightly a spout

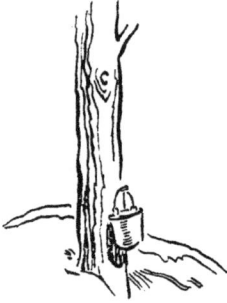

or spile, which can be purchased at the hardware store. Now hang upon the spout a small pail and at once you will see almost a miracle. Here is the proverbial "milk and honey" right in your own backyard. As the bucket fills, carry it inside to the iron kettle. Set it to boil as you would the tea kettle. As it boils down add more sap. Before too long the liquid will take on a bright light amber color. First-run syrup of the highest grade is judged on its weight and color. The browner syrup color seems to depend on the seasonal variation. To test for right consistency, instruments have been invented which measure specific gravity. Do not let this disturb you. Our grandfathers had a simpler method that worked. They used just plain "horse sense." When the syrup begins to thicken, put a drop of it between your thumb and first finger. Feel for stickiness. It should feel like light mucilage. Another test is to lift a spoonful of syrup and watch it flow. If it flows like water, boil it some more. If it flows like a salad oil or light honey, it is ready for bottling. Seal it in sterile jars. The womenfolk will know how to handle hot syrup and hot bottles, filling them until they overflow. You will look with pride in the months ahead on this stored-up-life-giving energy which can serve to dress up many a meal. Hot biscuits, fried cornmeal, hot cereals, french toast, ice cream, puddings and all manner of pancakes, waffles and fritters are enhanced with this sweetest of sweets.

Some of my happiest boyhood recollections go back to "Sugarin' ". We had a thousand or more maple trees. This required a sugar house with a sap pan four feet by ten and about five inches deep. The pan was built or set upon brick walls which served to hold the wood fire. A chimney rose from the end farthest from the door. Our sugarhouse was made of logs, unchinked, to allow the steam from the boiling to make its escape. A cupola top directly over the pans was open on all sides to allow for additional escape of steam. It was located on the side of a hill so that the stone boat with its four-hundred-gallon barrel for gathering sap was able to deliver its load to the storage tank well below the road but above the level of the boiling vats. No one had to carry sap uphill. One man drove the oxen with whip and a flow of wild language. Sap gathering was strictly men's work, and powerful language and chewing tobacco were in vogue. Some of the men boasted shooting a stream of tobacco juice fifteen feet, never missing the mark by two inches. These energies might have been directed into better channels, but in those primitive days

men had to assert themselves by existing standards and the top ones handled their chewing tobacco with a nicety.

My buddy, "Nicki," an Indian boy, and I hitchhiked on the tail end of the stone boat while two hired men, one on either side of the tank, trotted to the trees for the full sap buckets; replaced them with empty ones, running back and forth to the slow moving stone boat to empty their loads. The years of logging and sugaring had worn rude trails through the trees. In a year of abundant flow, one thousand buckets had to be emptied each day of the run. It was Uncle Claude's job to keep up the fires to keep the vats and pans boiling, boiling, boiling. The steam was so thick one couldn't see the length of the sugar house. These were no eight-hour days. We stayed with the job as long as the sap ran. It was satisfying. We felt rich and prosperous, with little concern about tomorrow. The good earth was giving generously. This fine flow meant profits as well as added home comforts.

When darkness fell and the last trip through the trees was hauled in, the real fun of sugarin' began. Usually we were early-to-bed folks, but at sap time the lid was off. Neighbors drifted in and out to taste and chat. As the syrup began to form in the syrup pan, it was ladled off just for fun. We dripped it over a pan of clean packed snow. It congealed in sticky strands that could be wound on smooth sticks or forks and munched like soft taffy.

Each winter we revive the thrilling memories with sugar on snow — made in a kitchen. When the mood suited, or when Ken thought to bring his mouth organ, there was singing — such harmony — such "barbershop" minors — such spirit. Sometimes it was a planned party with home-made bread, and ham roasted in the coals. The sharpy salty flavor was a nice contrast to the rich sweetness. There were eggs hardboiled in the sap. Broiled bits of salt pork and bacon.

When the happy crowd recalled the program of their own tomorrows, they left us. The menfolk who must stay 'til the syrup was run into the new shiny cans, settled down to a game of pedro or casino. The cards were extracted from between two logs. They stuck together a bit, but we didn't mind. It was all part of the game.

So when February comes along, let's make syrup. If you haven't a maple tree, look for the mists rising over the maple groves in the nearby country. Any farmer will enjoy sharing the fun of his Sugarin' with you. Just as the golden syrup is yours for the taking, so is the friendliness of shared experience. We can still use today these solid friendly values.

Cooking
Contraptions

Cooking Contraptions

Dan Boone not only hiked through, but cooked his way across "Kaintuck," often under the most trying circumstances. Quite likely he lived on jerked venison, dried meats, smoked fish and wild roots and berries. When he was fortunate enough to find friendly Indians or backwoods settlers, he no doubt gorged himself — thinking, "Well, I can eat scantily now for quite a spell." I'm sure, too, he enjoyed a fairly well-balanced meal of his own providing, when he felt secure from lurking enemies and could afford time to set up camp for a while. Fish from the nearby stream, a rabbit, wild turkey, even a porcupine. He always carried flour or cornmeal, salt and fat (bacon or bear grease). I'm sure he didn't eat just to live on these occasions, but enjoyed that quiet outdoor meal of his own choosing. Wild greens, red or black raspberries — he must have picked a noggin full of them.

The noggin has a rich history in America. It's just a drinking cup made of gnarled wood. It's taken from the burl of a hardwood tree, usually a sugar maple. The burl results from

NOGGIN WITH
BELT TOGGLE

153

nature's attempt to heal the scar of a branch broken off at the trunk of the tree by a storm or high wind. The result is a large "wart," the burl, which protrudes four to six inches from the tree. It is cup shaped and can be cut or sawed off to form the noggin. With a gouging tool the inside is dug out — tediously, carefully, because the burl is knotty with cross-grained and interlocking fibres. With skill and patience, it can be trimmed down to the thickness of a china cup. It is then boiled in linseed oil becoming very hard and tough as leather. A hole is bored near the lip, through which is drawn a leather thong for fastening to the belt. When one of these early pioneers wanted to express friendship for another fellow, he'd fashion a noggin for him. This was indeed a gift. Did you ever try to drink without a cup?

Today our outdoor cooking takes us back to the same thoughts of freedom, the same delights of blended smoke and frost fragrance, the same eager appetite. We've added, of course, a few conveniences, refinements.

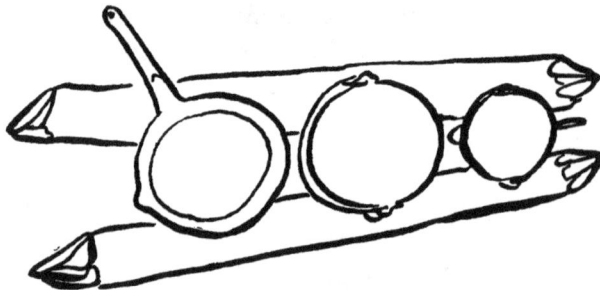

MODERN REVIVALS

This simple outdoor fireplace is easily constructed if you have stones. You do not need plaster or cement. It can be laid up just like a stone wall is laid. If you have clay on your land, it will serve perfectly as a binder. The cost involved will be a grate. With this type of open fireplace it is best to let your fire-wood burn until you have a thick bed of coals before placing your cooking utensils on the grate. This will avoid a lot of pot-black on your kettles from the smoke.

The outdoor fireplace with the chimney is really the best for all-round efficiency. Build the chimney at least six feet high. It will carry the smoke above your head; especially if the wind is contrary. Standing in front of an open fire, your body somehow acts as a chimney wall and the smoke will travel toward you and of course, get into your eyes and lungs. So the chimney on your outdoor fireplace is worth the time and effort it takes to build it.

Chimney construction in an outdoor fire-place is indeed simple. It does not call for any of the rules required in building a fireplace in your cabin. An inside fireplace is more or less draft controlled. It burns best when all doors and windows are closed. There is usually enough seepage of air from cabin windows and doors to supply a slight flow of air to the fireplace. Opening a window just a half-inch will help in the circulation and air flow. Then, too, the inside fireplace must be correctly built; i.e. smoke shelf just inside and below the flue; also smoke pockets. There is an exact relationship of the throat to the opening of your fireplace.

In the outdoor fireplace you need not be concerned with these building precautions. All you need is the fire pit and a flue large enough to carry off the smoke.

The grate covering your ash pit should be eighteen inches wide by twenty-four inches deep. The front of the chimney should start at the far end of the grate. In my own outdoor fireplace I have added a 3/16 inch steel plate eighteen by twenty-four inches. Here we have the same as the top of a kitchen stove without the pot holes. With this steel plate cover, the draft travels in from the front through the fire pit and up the chimney. The steel plate has the added value of keeping your kettles free from smoke. It will give ample heat for all cooking except for broiling your steaks. To broil steaks or chops remove the steel plate and your bed of hot coals under the grate should be perfect to roast your meat . . . rare, medium or well done.

At this point the coals in the fire pit no longer need any draft. Instead of building a damper within your chimney, a simple device will do just as well and again without cost. Just a piece of tin or sheet iron placed on top of the chimney flue will immediately shut off all draft. If there is still smoke from bits of burning wood just slide the tin damper a bit to one side to allow the smoke to escape.

If there is danger of fire during dry summer weather when sparks from your fireplace may give you concern, you can control this by placing a wire screen on top of your chimney flue. Weigh it down with a few small stones. If your fire burns too wildly in a situation like this you can quickly discipline it wth a cup or two of cold water.

MAKE IT ATTRACTIVE

While the mechanics of outdoor fireplace construction are important, let us also put into the building a bit of simple artistry. There should be ample shelf space. A big stone slab on either side of the fire pit. Shelves near the chimney. They will serve also as warming ovens. After a little experience you will find the right spots to keep your plates hot, another to keep the coffee simmering. Add to this a stone seat or two. A bit of rail fence will invite birds and small animals. The stone slabs on either side of your fire pit will, with constant use, become covered with grease and pot black and will show discoloration. This is easily removed by simply sprinkling a thin coat of wood ashes over the greasy part. The lye in the ashes will take up the grease. Brush off and scrub as you would your kitchen sink. Your stone will sparkle again with its natural color and look most inviting.

Here we have a deluxe adaptation of the outdoor cooking place with a roof. I have seen some very elaborate housed-in "cooking contraptions" which left me with the feeling, "Why after all forsake the efficient kitchen in the house?" The only advantage of a roof is in the event of a sudden rainstorm after you have gotten the meal underway. I've met this problem with an eight-foot square canvas which can be quickly placed.

Cooking out-of-doors with a roof overhead and then side walls and what-not, is no longer out-of-doors. We just shut out the sky, interrupt passing breezes. We build a semi-civilized situation that defeats what we started out to do—to build and live with an outdoor cooking contraption.

SMOKE HOUSE

After walking home two miles from our
one-room country school, there were two or
three things in mother's larder to quicken my
step. In the fall there were fish hanging in the
smoke house—fish which we caught with nets in
our nearby river. These would smoke and sizzle
for several days. They would shrink thinner
and thinner as the smoke and heat would play
on them. I would sink my teeth into one of
these until I'm sure I had grease from ear to
ear. This "ceremony" next led to the ten-gal-
lon dill pickle jar—a great big juicy sour dill

pickle, topped off with a great slice of home-made bread. By that time I was really ready to do justice to one of mother's bountiful meals. We never failed to have one or two big jars full of dill pickles each fall. Nothing much to making these. The bundle of dried dill which had been hanging in the woodshed was brought down and spread as a thin matting on the bottom of the jar. Then each green cucumber was washed and wrapped in a grape leaf. (Here I am inclined to wander, to tell you about our winery where we made grape juice and set a keg to fermenting for special winter occasions.) After the layer of cucumbers covered the matting of dill, a handful of salt was spread; then again more dill, more wrapped cucumbers and so on until the jar was full. Mother used to pour on added salt-water each day after skimming off the froth and scum which gathered on the top of the jar.

Now here I am talking about pickles when I started on smoke houses! Besides smoked fish, we had smoked hams, slabs of bacon, link sausages. I've missed the smoke house all the years I have been forced to live in the city. I really plan to have one again on my land. For smoke we used mostly hickory sawdust, small bark. It depends mostly what locality you live in. Your local meat dealer will quite likely have a smoke house of his own and if he does, I'm sure he has a big following. I'll walk a mile any time to find a dealer who still uses the old-fashioned method of the smoke house.

161

THE CAULDRON

The cauldron was indeed a cooking contraption of early history. Perhaps the first utilitarian cooking kettle created since men wrought iron. Shakespeare tied it with a "witches' toil and trouble brew." Indeed literature is full of incidents concerning the queer concoctions brewed in it. There is still something fascinating about this great kettle swung over an outdoor fire — giving off great waves of steam and varied odors from its wildly boiling contents.

In early American days no household was complete without a cauldron. To inherit the family cauldron was a highly desired bequest. To the women folk it was a far handier tool than the electric washer of today. The men folks returning from the fields with oxen and stone-boat, never failed to pick up all trash wood, fallen branches, pieces of broken rail-fence to provide a good supply of firewood to keep the cauldron going. On Mondays the cauldron was used by grandmother for boiling the weekly washing. On butchering days, when hogs were to be prepared for winter, it was sometimes necessary to borrow a second kettle. Some of them weigh several hundred pounds, have to be rolled on a stone-boat and pulled by oxen. Often the neighbors came along to help and to join in the fun, exchange of gossip and "politickin' ". Grandfather had the rigging ready the night before; at least two scaffoldings, one for swinging the great cauldrons over the fire, for great quantities of scalding water were needed for this ceremony. Then, too, there was the scaffolding with pulley attached to hoist the dressed hogs high and then drop them into the huge barrel or "hogs-head" of boiling hot water in preparation for scrubbing and thorough cleaning. A crude table was built for quartering the hog and preparing for winter. Little of the hog was wasted by those thrifty folks. Grandpa used to say, "We save everything but the squeal."

In early March the cauldron was used for boiling sap into maple syrup. As the boiling syrup reached the right consistency to be drawn off, it would suddenly foam and proceed to boil over. Never daunted, the cooks had a trick to save the day. A piece of fat pork tied to a string was quickly dropped into the froth. The overflow would subside. "Just pouring oil on the troubled waters," Grandma used to say. More than this, syrup in those days just did not taste right without the distinctive flavor of smoked bacon in it.

Along in the spring, too, came soap making and, in between the weekly washing (couldn't be too fussy in those days). They had to use the cauldron for food, syrup making, butchering. It was cleaned after each using; was thoroughly scrubbed with soft soap, scalded and turned upside down until it was needed again.

Modern varieties of utensils have caused the old cauldron to fall into disuse today and yet I would not part with the three-foot one which I own and which stands idle on my acres much of the time. Occasionally I loan it to my neighbor for his butchering. We sometimes use it for boiling a great mess of sweet corn. We still plan to cook a shore dinner in it someday. I rather like to feel that if gas and electricity should be turned off, if economics should be temporarily upset, if store shelves should again be empty, I could with my good axe cut my own wood; with my cauldron and other primitive gear we own, we could still maintain ourselves independently.

HOMEMADE SOAP

It seems almost incongruous to talk about making soap at home when one need but run to the corner to buy all kinds and qualities. So it was once. The recent war taught us better. Many of us had to cut our rations. Sometimes clothes could not be thoroughly washed. Even at the washstand, we used a quarter-cake just to be saving.

I also discovered that many folks resorted to making their own soap, just as our forebears used to do, but not so laboriously. Today it is cooked on the kitchen stove. It is quite simple. You don't have to get your lye from a lye vat. It now comes in tin cans from your drug or grocery store. Save all fat and put in a stone crock—pork rinds, ham fat—indeed all fats. When you have six pounds or more, place on stove to simmer until all grease floats and solid particles have dropped to bottom. Then pour off. Now empty the can of lye into an iron kettle to dissolve in about twelve quarts of water. Add the clear, clean grease after it has cooled. Boil all this slowly for three to five hours. If the contents boil down, keep adding water to maintain same level in kettle. At the end of boiling add eight ounces of salt—the impurities, as well as the excess water, will separate from the soap. There you have it! As it cools, it is poured into a low cardboard box, or make one of heavy paper, about one and a half inches deep. Cut in squares to fit the hand and set away to dry. (You will find instructions on how to make soap at home, on the can of lye from your store.)

Not so easy in the old days, but these pioneers would have their soap and they cooked it in the family cauldron. Lye for it was made from hardwood ashes. A barrel with holes bored into it near the bottom was placed on a flat stone drain board, slightly slanting toward the front. Into the surface of this stone had been chiseled grooves which carried the drippings from the barrel into a stone crock. Three to four pails of water were poured over the wood ashes which had been accumulating in the barrel. The resultant liquid was lye. The good old pioneers had no scientific method of measuring the quality of lye, but they were never stumped. If the lye could float an egg, or if the lye would eat the feathers from a quill, it was strong enough and it was good lye.

Into the lye was poured the waste fat saved throughout the year. It was put over the fire to boil and stirred with a sassafras stick to add a bit of fragrance—declared "done" when the liquid had thickened sufficiently to cling to the paddle.

I know a spot in Georgia where soap is still being made in a cauldron, where lye is still dripped from hardwood ash. Some day I'm going to hie me off to that spot—just for the fun of living over again soap-making as I remember it from my boyhood days.

Outdoor Menus

Outdoor Menus

Cooking in the outdoors can be fun for host and guests alike only if you learn to use a bit of showmanship—and if the results are well cooked—and served hot.

You will probably have to live through an experimental phase as I did. I have never lived down the time I poured a cup of salt into the breakfast cereal instead of a teaspoonful. There have been times also when too hot a fire almost ruined the bacon—and cheese dreams. But do not be discouraged; the acquired skill is worth the effort for the shared fun it brings.

After all a good cook has to tend to his cooking anywhere it is done. In an open outdoor fireplace the fire is less easily controlled. Soon you will learn to place your coffee-pot on the outer edge of your fire rather early in the game. You'll discover that eggs will do better if you place the frying pan on a few coals raked forward and away from the real heat of your fire. You will need more water than usual for your hunter's stew as it boils vigorously and can be left to itself for an hour or two only if

the water is sufficient to prevent it from boiling dry. Since I like to be part of the party, and at the same time near my cooking, I built my fireplace in the yard where my guests will gather and can share in the fun.

To prove yourself a dainty and clean cook remember to include in your nearby equipment a wash basin, soap and water, and a clean towel. For showmanship and to avoid burning from heat and steam, I like to wear, or have at hand, white canvas gloves.

And speaking of handy equipment, it does not add to the comfort of your family and guests to be constantly saying, "Oh, Mother, we forgot the salt," or "Mary, did you remember the soup ladle?" If you really want to enjoy your cooking enterprise, it is important to have all the utensils, ingredients, dishes, etc. carried out to your fireplace and arranged handily nearby before you start the ceremony. In the picture of our own family camp arrangement

The Author's Family Camp

you will notice that the kitchen division is efficiently arranged. There is an ice box for keeping cool things cool, a warming shelf for keeping hot things hot, a work shelf below the cupboard that contains spices and other cooking needs. Pans, spoons, forks and the like are accessible. All of this arrangement added to management assures results pleasurable to all.

KABOB AND TWIST

Perhaps the simplest meal is meat (beef, pork, lamb) on a sharpened stick, broiled over a small bed of hot coals. With this we serve biscuits made of flour, baking powder, salt and shortening, watered to a stiff paste, wrapped around a one-inch stick, and baked below your meat-stick. Add a cup of cocoa and an apple for dessert.

CHARCOAL STOVE

If firewood is not plentiful, try the charcoal stove. Just a round piece of sheet iron, or stovepipe, six inches in diameter and about six-

Kabob and Twist

171

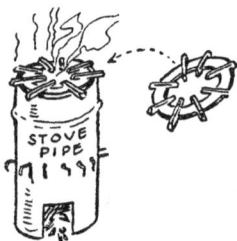

teen inches high. Add a wire fuel grate about four inches from the bottom, punching holes all around for holding the wires. Add an extra opening near the base for draft. Do all this with a pair of tin-snips, a pair of pliers and an ice-pick.

Now on the top lay a small grate. If mother doesn't see you, the removable grate of the kitchen gas stove will do nicely. A bit of paper and chips to start the fire, then fill the stove with charcoal. Face the draft-opening toward the wind and soon the coals will be red-hot and your stove ready for your cooking.

Here you can prepare a kettle of soup, fry wieners, eggs or hamburgers — with little fuss and few dishes to wash.

HAMBURGERS

Speaking of hamburgers, I've grown thoroughly dissatisfied with the modern hamburgers as served by most food shops. To begin with, they come paper-thin — almost as thin as the oil-paper sheets that separate them. They are then almost burned to a crisp, cooked through and through and served with hot sauces to cover the lack of natural flavor. Beef, to me, must always be rare at its heart. Try rare hamburgers. First buy good beef and have it chopped. Make it into small balls, or fat patties two inches thick. Put a little butter into the frying pan. Be sure your fire is *hot*. Fry vigorously for two minutes. Flatten slightly. Turn, season and repeat. Your hamburger is ready to serve. It is as good as a choice steak — costs less and is most simple to prepare. It's fun!

HUNTER'S STEW

If you want to serve a meal to a large group without spending half of next month's earnings, try "Kettle-Hole Hunter's Stew." It is easily prepared and makes a satisfying meal. It's unique and different.

Let's say you are to have ten or fifteen folks for Sunday supper. Buy boneless meat — beef, lamb, pork — or all three. Allow six ounces per person. Bones will add to the richness and flavor but should not be counted on as fillers. Cut the meat into small pieces and drop into hot salted water. You will not have to watch your Kettle Hole stew, but can return after two hours and find it ready to serve. Here's how.

Dig a hole about eighteen inches deep and six inches wider than the diameter of your cooking utensil. We use a ten-quart pail with a lid. Be sure the walls of the pit are straight up and down. Now set a crotched stick on either side of the hole. Across these lay a green pole. Hang the pail to the cross-pole so that it is half way down into the hole. Before plac-

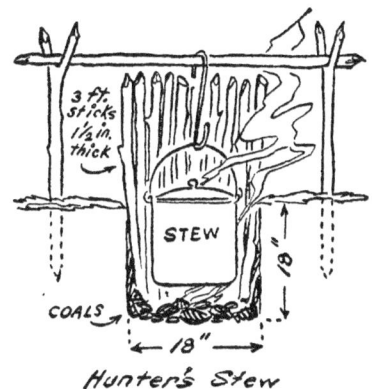

Hunter's Stew

ing the pail, build a good fire in the hole. Let it burn until a bed of live coals has accumulated. Now place your pail filled three-quarters full of water. Next build a stockade fence of three-foot-length branches (about one to three inches in thickness) around the pail. See that the lower ends of these branches are resting in the coals below. Your fire is now self-feeding.

When the water boils, salt it and add your meat. Then leave it alone. Bring out the camp chairs and cushions. Do your "politickin'" and savor the fragrance of your stew. Control your appetite. Just a half-hour before serving, add vegetables — potatoes, carrots, celery, onions, seasoning. When all is ready, ladle out a cup of broth, add a crisp salad, bread and butter, a light dessert, coffee. You'll like it. Your guests will go home well fed and happy, and will be eager to try this easy meal in their own backyards.

POTATOES BAKED IN A HOLE

The earth must be sandy and reasonably dry. Potatoes will bake brown and mealy in fifty-five minutes in a fire hole. Dig the hole eighteen inches deep by fourteen wide. Build a fire of hardwood. Let it burn until the hole is half full of coals. With a shovel push the coals aside, throw in a layer of potatoes. Quickly release the shovel and the potatoes will be covered with hot coals. Now fill in the hole with the loose dirt which has been dug out from the hole. The potatoes cannot char, but will come out brown and mealy.

Another way is to wrap the potatoes in clay and bake in the coals of a campfire. About the same time is required. A few experiments are necessary to prove this skill.

NEW ENGLAND BOILED DINNER

Just which of the New England States would claim discovery of this richly flavored meal, I do not know. It came to me from our Vermont relatives and shared the honors with Boston Baked Beans and Brown Bread as a Saturday night repast.

The unit is a lean rump of freshly corned beef. It is covered with cold water and set to simmer in a large covered kettle. After an hour or so (depending, of course, on the weight of the piece), the vegetables are added. First (because they take most time), add golden slices of turnip or rutabaga. Then add quarters of young cabbage, about three large onions and as many whole potatoes as desired. No further salt or seasoning is necessary. Now in a separate kettle set to simmer until tender, plenty of fresh red beets. Cook them with their jackets on to preserve their deep-red color. Serve these separately. (Don't peel beets with a knife. As soon as they are cool enough to handle, jackets can be gently squeezed off.)

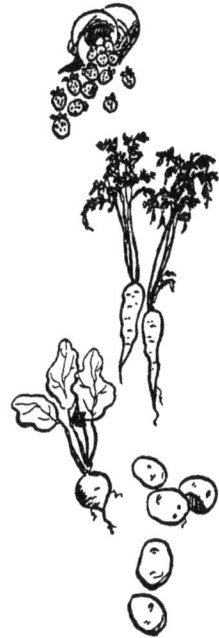

175

"RED FLANNEL" HASH

After your New England dinner, drain all vegetables thoroughly. Remove the corned beef. Add to the drained vegetables the peeled beets. Place in a wooden chopping bowl. Chop fine and mix thoroughly. Let stand overnight and serve for breakfast. Just heat thoroughly in a buttered frying pan or skillet. This meal has become a standard Sunday morning breakfast with us.

CHILI

There is one meal we like to serve on any occasion where food and simple preparation are the two points most in focus. It is the kind of a meal, too, which can be stretched almost indefinitely. It is easily carried, easily salvaged. It is a one-dish meal with all the needed food elements. Its preparation need take a mere twenty minutes and yet, what is often more important in a mixed group of varied plans and interests, it never spoils by a delay in serving.

The unit ingredients serve five. Into an iron-covered kettle place one pound of hamburger. Cover it and let it sear rather than brown. Add one large can of tomatoes, one jar of prepared kidney beans, one can of spaghetti in spicy sauce. Add a heaping teaspoon of salt. Stir well and let it heat through. Just before serving, add two tablespoonfuls of Chili powder.

If the group number has not been determined before the purchase of supplies, double the amount of hamburger, triple the number of cans and all is set for 'most any contingency, provided the kettle space is adequate. Add a quarter-pound of hamburger and one can of any of the ingredients for each additional guest. Somehow, though the flavor may be varied slightly in one direction or another, it won't ruin the nourishing and appetizing result. The unopened cans, even the unused hamburger can be utilized for other meals without waste.

BAKED BEANS

Here is a bit of outdoor bean cookery that works. Baked beans like mother used to make. Beans are put to soak overnight and then boiled until tender. They are then placed in a stone jar with cover. The jar is then filled with chunks of salt pork, syrup, spice to suit one's taste. For an oven, use a five-gallon tin can with the top removed or a piece of sheet iron the height of the stone jar and about three feet long, bent into a circle to fit around the jar. Cover the top with a piece of flat tin. A slow-burning fire built around the tin cover is the last step, except to dip into the jar from time to time to taste and to keep enough water on the beans to prevent burning. But "what a meal" when the pork and beans are served!

HOE CAKE

Since my mother was born and raised on a plantation near Augusta, Georgia, I have a fondness for the Sunny South, its folks and friendly ways. In our Northern home we have enjoyed many of the stories of plantation life and have indulged in and enjoyed many southern dishes — biscuits such as only southerners can make — corn pones — hoe cake.

It was not until recent years that I had a real demonstration of Hoe Cake cooking by a Negro Mammy. It appears that hoe cake had its origin among the Negroes, who, when short of cooking utensils, used the garden hoe as a griddle in the fireplace. The recipe is still the same, but a frying pan is far superior to the hoe. *HOE CAKE* (for six people)

Ingredients: 3 cups cornmeal, 1½ tsps. salt, 4 cups of milk, handful of raisins.

Mix thoroughly. Then add 1 cup flour to give consistency, 2 tbsp. sugar, 8 tsp. fat. Bake over glowing hot coals.

PERPETUAL PANCAKES

Ingredients: 3 cups of buckwheat flour, ½ tsp. salt, 1 yeast cake (in first mixing), 2 cups buttermilk, or sour milk, or water, 1 tsp. baking soda.

This unit can be varied according to the number of pancakes desired. There should be at least a cupful of batter left as a starting unit for the next day. Again add milk, flour or cornmeal.

CORN PONES
(for eight people)

Ingredients: 3 cups yellow cornmeal, 1 cup flour, 1 tsp. salt, 8 tsps. baking powder, 2 tsp. sugar, 4 cups water.

Combine dry ingredients and shortening. Stir in enough water to be able to drop mixture from spoon.

To bake: (1) Fill pan ½ inch deep and place in reflector oven; or,

(2) Put batter in frying pan, ¼ inch thick —hold over fire to bake bottom. Then bake top by reflector heat—propping pan agains fire; or (3) Drop spoonfuls on very hot rock.

LYE HOMINY

There is nothing more delicious than hominy made from field corn. Fried hominy for breakfast is better than brown-fried potatoes. We always used lye from ashes made in our own leach, never commercial lye. One-half gallon of shelled corn, two gallons or more of water, lye enough to turn corn red. Boil until skin and little black ends slip off. Wash thoroughly and the skins will float off the pail. Then boil until tender. Keep covered in water.

179

PICNIC A LA CART

Try out your guests on a party "picnic a la cart." This is a small, two-wheeled cart with icebox, storage room for food, fixings and cooking gear. All spaces are arranged for the picnic feed. Make it yourself. I made mine and it works. It is different.

Two drop-leaf tables that fold on top when open, give ample serving space. You don't have to go to your backyard fireplace every time you want an outdoor meal. If on a stream or lake, or at the seashore, have a shore dinner — clams, lobsters. Start off with clam broth or soup. Try hot dogs or a New England dinner with vegetables.

If you have a favorite spot, a view from a hilltop, a sunset — perhaps a swim — then load your "Picnic a la Cart," food, drinks and gear and have a hilltop meal with inspirational view. It will give you a different setting. Your friends will like it and beg to come again.

"Picnic a la Cart" is a country home variety to your place in the woods. It's just a stunt; but different. It is the "tea tray" in your living room, a bit roughed up. It's fun. It's novel. Add a few cushions, a camp-fire, songs, stunts, the moon, twinkling stars . . . a perfect party.

Free Enterprise

Free Enterprise

We are the strongest nation on earth today because our pioneer forefathers worked for
it. What about tomorrow? We must not forget that we owe our strength to what we have
kept of the courage, resourcefulness and imagination of our pioneers who were willing to
give of themselves. We, too, must keep our
feet planted firmly in the good earth, in the
philosophy of that thinking. We must keep
our faith in simple things. We need only to
adapt this whole simple chain of philosophy to
meet the new conditions of living today. I hope
these pages may help us not to forget our
American heritage, the gift of our forefathers
— free enterprise, hard work, thrift and working with God. As free men we can continue today to make it happen.

But, Partner, I grow too serious for such a
day — or is it on a day in a spot like this that
we see most clearly the needs and yearnings of
folks? I am completely satisfied that most
people in America are really pioneers in spirit
and that they want to hold on to the great

simple traditions that made America great. These are the folk who love the good earth, who believe in honest effort and who have found and kept a sane, deep working faith in God.

If I can create a new and different mouse-trap and folks come to my door to buy it and will pay me enough for my labor, plus something more for my creativeness, I call that free enterprise and yet free to "render unto Caesar those things that are Caesar's." We need but to review the American ingenuity to realize what a creative, bargaining, bartering people our forefathers were. They were good horse traders. Carried passengers in small sail boats along the Atlantic coast for a stated fare. Dams were built and grist mills opened on many small streams that could turn water wheels. They built canals to improve transportation but, also, always with an eye for profits. Then railroads — and the first steam boat. Free enterprise developed American ingenuity, the skill to create and sell and make a profit. Free enterprise started on the land.

Most of these have passed into professional and commercial hands and have developed into great national industries. All of them had their beginning, indeed, simple beginning on the farm where by the "trial and error" method we learned how.

If there was need to do it again, we could. These early experiences have left planted in the heart of America that free enterprise is still ours. The freedom to dream, create; to build

184

things that people want — things to make life easier against those early days of hard work. It's the American way of getting on in the world.

In those early days on the farm we were many factories in one — home canning, bread making in home-made ovens, damp vegetable cellars now replaced by electric refrigeration, soap making, maple syrup and sugar — even the tanning and curing of hides.

On the farm with free enterprise we just worked and took things from Mother Nature. Our garden supplied us in abundance, rich abundance — all manner of vegetables, strawberries, budding asparagus, radishes, celery, carrots, beets and beet-tops. In early spring we picked dandelions, fresh and green for salads. Horseradish roots dug up winter or summer for hot spice. Also many other wild plants and plant life. Then, too, wild berries from the hills, red and black raspberries. Of course in the spring there was the hunting season for Mallards, Wild Duck, on Lake Winnebago. These all dressed and prepared and packed in tubs of lard by the women folks and served on winter nights. We had them for the taking. Later we had Golden Bantam corn, potatoes and root vegetables. In the fall, hickory nuts, hazelnuts, beechnuts, butter-nuts. We made picnics on these occasions to gather nuts. Then the hunting season for deer and an occasional black bear. I still like the taste of bear grease. Venison, bear meat dressed and hung in the hay barn to cure. Skins, too, were preserved

White Birch

Beech

for floor mats or made into moccasins for house wear. The sheep supplied us wool as well as mutton. Mother always had a dozen quilts of carded wool, tightly stitched and neatly hemmed and stored away for extra cover on those zero nights, and for the added guests. Down feathers were plucked from the breasts of geese each year, washed and dried and stored in bags to be made some day into pillows that really invited peaceful sleep. Ashes from the kitchen stove were carefully hoarded and stored in the lye vat from which later we made our homemade soap and lye hominy. The smoke house in the backyard gave that rich flavor to hams, slabs of bacon, pork sausages, great tubs full of fish we caught with nets in spawning season in the Menomenee River. Maple syrup and maple sugar made from our own trees supplied our sweets — all this from the good earth.

Free enterprise. We just went into business by ourselves; created all manner of things; raised the fruits from the land that men lived by and sold them, and when we had little to sell or barter and times grew hard, well, we took it on the chin, but not for long. Somehow we got by, but prepared better the next year for family security.

I would not ask of life today the hard, cruel struggle of these early folks of ours. Modern devices have made living easier, thank God. But if these devices make us soft — then God help us. Too many soft people in this country

of ours will make a soft America. Softness is accepted weakness. Softness, and weakness produce schemers, cheaters, quislings and ultimate losers.

Black Cherry

At Home
In The Forest

At Home in the Forest

Did you ever have that empty feeling when by yourself in the deep woods, when eerie noises from the wild life, the movement of trees and bushes gave you a bit of jitters and the sense of utter aloneness? I have lived through that experience but have outgrown it. Now the woods are full of friendliness. I have learned to know the wild folk by name and nature and noises that have simple homely meanings. The squirrel scolds. The chipmunk chirps. The crow calls "Caw, caw, caw," a rally or a warning.

Look about you. You will discover three worlds teeming with abundant life. Beneath you — the underground world — small holes in the earth, home and security to hundreds of small animals. A world from which man is barred. Backdoors and frontdoors, storage rooms and communication tunnelings. Then there is a world for the long-legs that depend

191

on speed for their livelihood. They step noiselessly, creep stealthily, or crash boldly through the trails or brush, according to their natures. The fox, the wolf, the deer — not often seen by the white man who has never learned the art of stalking, who cannot avoid snapping twigs, who "telegraphs" ahead of his approach as he brushes and stirs dry leaves in passing.

The third world is that of the treetops and the sky. Here squirrels use the interwoven branches as their natural thoroughfare. Song birds flit from tree to tree, hawks circle and swoop, wild geese in patterned flight thread seemingly charted paths across the dark blue ocean of the sky.

Man is never alone in the woods. Even at night you can see the gleam of tiny eyes watching you, fearful, ever alert. The satisfying triumph of their confidence in you is worth the time and patience it takes to win.

LOST AND FOUND

Being lost either in the woods, or the city, or anywhere else for that matter, can be largely attributed to just plain ignorance. The uninformed get lost. The would-be sailor who takes a sailboat out in a light breeze becomes "lost" when the fog descends and he realizes he is not wise in the ways of the water.

Being lost is closely allied to being confused. Confusion comes from lack of pertinent information.   How often we meet people who join in discussion "over their heads" and find themselves utterly "lost" because they were misinformed or uninformed.

But let's talk of being lost in the woods. When one loses one's sense of direction, one becomes confused, then frantic and apt to do very silly things.   To cringe in the presence of a black snake is to be "lost" in the woods.   To know good snakes from bad is to know that a black snake is as tame and playful as a kitten. It is an unwise man who tampers with wild mushrooms.   Many have paid the full price for ignorance.

When in doubt, sit down on a log, take time and bring your best reasoning to bear. You will soon get your bearing.   A good woodsman entering a thick woods, stops occasionally to look back, realizing that the way in and the way out will have different landmarks.   He breaks a branch here and there.   Leaves a stone or two at a turning point in the trail; watches the tree tops and notes each out-of-the-ordinary landmark.

THE BLIZZARD

In my boyhood days, I spent several November days in the woods of Northern Wisconsin with a trusted friend, Necktie Jim. He was a Winnebago Indian who loved the outdoors as I did. From him I learned pointed lessons on how *not* to be lost in the woods. I learned from him to take good or bad weather as it came, to live comfortably amidst the wild life, because he knew nature's secrets. He knew what wild plants were edible. He knew how to snare small animals and catch fish. I learned to watch, rather than ask foolish boy-questions. "Storm coming," Jim would say,

"Build tepee quick." "Storm coming," did not mean to Jim a passing change in the weather. It meant raging wind, driving rain or blasting snow and sleet. "Storm," to this day, is a meaningful word to me, not to be toyed with. I learned then that it called for preparation, quick action, to give safety from the elements.

On this particular trip in November, the weather had been mild until a big black cloud loomed in the western horizon. Jim and I had been in the woods for two days. We were about ten miles from the nearest farm house. I noticed that he was watching the sky. When he finally said, "Storm coming quick," I understood his laconic but impressive language and said obediently, "What shall I do?" "Get much wood," said Jim. This I did with alacrity, for I knew Necktie Jim knew that those darkening, driving, ominous clouds called for the first rules of self-preservation. I gathered branches large and small. Soon drifting, blinding snow proved his foreboding. I ran faster. I dared not stop. I sensed what lay in store for us — deep snow, freezing temperature. I must satisfy his intelligent command, "Get much wood." I was so occupied with my job, I did not notice what Jim was doing, but he had been busy. With his hatchet he had fashioned a pole between the crotch of two trees. Against this he had laid saplings, slanting toward the storm. Sacrificing one of our blankets for a wind break, he had covered it with small hemlock boughs, leaves and sod. Before the improvised

shelter he had built a glowing fire. By this time the snow was driving with an impact and force that made me realize we never could have gotten home that night, if we had tried to carry on. Here we were safe before a glowing fire. As he banked-in the corners, I saw that he had not forgotten to gather dry leaves and pine boughs for our bed — had even added to my store of firewood. This, you remember, was before the era of parks and cleared woodland. We were in the heart of virgin country, where firewood was plentiful.

Snug and safe, we were ravenously hungry. We took stock. A bag of raisins, one of cornmeal, a chunk of jerked venison, salt and a bit of bear grease. I have eaten meals at our leading hotels, I've banqueted on delicacies and unusual concoctions of high-priced chefs, but never have I had a meal so gorgeous, so entirely satisfying as this one prepared in a snow-storm by Necktie Jim.

Were we snug and warm that night in the blizzard? Did we get home safely the next day? Were my parents worried? Of course, my mother was anxious, as mothers will be, but not really worried. She knew Necktie Jim. To say we were "snug as a bug in a rug," would be silly, unless you and I both have the same definition for "snug." We were secure. We had the warmth of the fire on one side. We kept our blood in circulation by constantly tending the fire, plugging small drift-holes against the storm. We sat for a spell with our backs together for extra warmth.

To this day, I still like to use short sentences because of the influence of Jim. Each of his words had content and a very definite meaning. Though limited they imparted to me, as we lived their meaning, potent lessons that have served me well. When I hear folks today refer to a "pretty storm," I long again to be with Jim and observe the utter disgust expressed in his face as he listened to such chatter. I'm sure he might say, "White man make little talk."

I never had a million dollars and don't know what it feels like, but I had a lesson in security worth a million dollars that I learned from this Indian who could take nature in his stride, and could dismiss for all time the silly fear of being lost. The Indian philosophy is unique. "Me not lost. Tepee lost." So, we built ourselves another tepee from the natural resources at hand and were at home, not lost in the storm.

Woodland
Sounds

Woodland Sounds

There is no place in the whole wide world where one may find sweeter melodies than in the Great Out Doors. God composed the songs for nature and made them vocal. Away, far away from the man-made noises, woodland songs are recorded on the delicate auditory nerve — always rhythmic, satisfying, stirring, if we will only train ourselves to listen.

The clang of street-cars, the blare of automobile horns and sirens, the screech of brakes and tires — city noises have become so natural to us that we scarcely realize how they tighten our nerves and dull our ears to the delicate sounds of the outdoors. Indeed, the poignant stillness of one's first day in the woods may be oppressive and lonely. An afternoon is not long enough to establish the closeness, the desire necessary for a mood of receptiveness to what God's outdoors has to give. Men in the busy whirl of city life may not retreat long enough in the outdoors to find this great musical secret — indeed, phenomenon. It takes almost solitude for a few days — or away-ness with a companion with whom you are in tune. Tune

Shagbark Hickory

not only your ear, but yourself, to the quiet. Turn the dials of your human radio down, down to the wave length of the wind's whisper. It takes patience, relaxation, time, but the inspiration, the refreshment is worth it — and more! A new song world is yours for the taking. Zephyrs flowing through the trees, causing idle leaves to laughingly brush one another. Breezes and wind sigh or roar. It is a singing world we live in — from the trickling stream, the gurgling water as it falls over rocks, to mating songs of birdland and the wailing, warning and wooing calls of wild creatures. Even the grander sounds of the rhythmic pattern of pounding ocean waves and driving storm, have music.

Wind, in its many moods, is always musical. The varied names for the wind in its ever-changing tempo are in themselves musical. Zephyr, breeze, wind, — ring in the ear. Tempest, hurricane, cyclone, typhoon — dangerous in their import — yet sounds that are strong, vibrant, resonant. As a youngster, I used to call across the small valley on our farm, "Heigh-ho!" and "Heigh-ho" came back to me from the rocky cliff in that mystical echo of tempered tones. I called more softly, and the words came back to me no longer raucous, but quiet, reassuring and soothing. Grown-up I still trek back to the farm (long since in other hands), but the echo is still mine and returns "Heigh-ho" when I call. Ours is a singing world!

202

I despair today of the brash radio's "canned" noise. I say "noise," because when sounds are jumbled, discordant, meaningless, they are no longer sounds, but noises. Thomp-thomp - thomp - bass notes of South African voo-doo syncopated for the modern dance; croonings and commercial jingles, squeaks and dronings; screams and shots to add "color" to a bit of lurid mystery and drama. These are noises — not music.

Music had its beginning in the sounds of Nature's great outdoors — whispering winds, laughing springs, babbling brooks and rustling leaves — the deep notes of the croaking bull-frog, the hum of the bee, the high-pitched call of the goldfinch on the wing — the rumble and crash of thunder, the scream and roar of the windstorm. Wagner, Grieg, Tschaikovsky, Beethoven and the other immortals, through their magnificent symphonic music, have portrayed woodland sounds for man.

But we need not always go to man-made concerts for our inspiration. Sit on a tree stump and relax, without "fuss or feather," or the price of a front-row seat. Tune your ear to the song of the brook. Hark to the Meadow Lark as he welcomes spring from the fields still brown and dull. Listen to the Cat-bird's mimicry, the Cardinal's mellow whistle, the plaintive Mourning Dove and Hermit Thrush as they greet the twilight. Move to the edge of your lily pond, to the cheery assurance of the peepers. Drink deep the vibrant melodies of

Sycamore

an awakening world. Sit on your cabin veranda and enjoy the majestic sounds of the "Storm King," the gusts of wind singing as they rush through the trees. Note the homely sounds that a storm brings to life — the old hanging saw on the woodshed hums, the taut clothes line whines, a loose shingle or an overhanging branch beats rhythmically.

As a boy, I was once told of the "Master Violin Builder" who created a giant violin by stretching wires across a great valley and pulling them taut. Nary a sound from them until the gentle breeze increased into gale velocity. As harder and harder it blew, there came from the strings a heavenly harmony of sound and song, mild and deep tones mingled with those on high, until heaven sang forth a great symphony and men who heard it were lifted and inspired.

So tune your ear to the simple and beautiful music of woodland sounds. God composed these songs to lift men's hearts — if they will but listen.

Sweet Gum

The Mirror of
My Pond

The Mirror of My Pond

There is nothing wrong with
God and His green earth!

Sitting on the bank of my small pond, I see the trees and hills beyond reflected in the quiet water. The day is still, almost breathless. On the far bank idles a fawn. I watch the mirror of this little sea; the fawn is standing upside down on the far bank; the trees and hills, too, reach deep into the dark water. All is in reverse. Like the world today, too many things seem upside down — reversed. We despair, even though we know the world is not really so — only made to appear so by our own perversity.

Look up, look up, Brother. The treetops and the skyline of the hills quickly right themselves. They never were in reverse. The fawn is erect, grazing and nibbling as deer have done since creation. God's world can be counted on. It is a good world. In man's viewpoint lies the difference. To often we see darkness, despair, doubt, dark reflections of the world rather than its reality, its hope and promise.

In your childhood days did you ever look through the wrong end of a telescope? We search for the truth through the wrong end of the telescope. We see only little men and not the truth. We search for the shadows and not the light. We miss the sunshine and so fail to find the hope, the success, the spirit created by God in our fellowman.

Let us look to the hills for our inspiration, search in the outdoors for His truth, remembering that each year God's green earth blossoms and comes to fruit. This is truth. Will we ever learn? So, Brother, look up. Lift your sights. Search for the loftiness in man — all men — and you will find no dark reflections. Face into the morning sun beyond your pond to the hills beyond and see bright and warming reflections of life. Face the challenge of a better life. Go with the belief that all men are born free and equal. Each, according to his own talents, is free to make his place in the world, as a free man equal among men — the owner of the right to vote, to live his own life. Face the morning sun that casts its warming rays on all men — whatever their religious or political beliefs, whatever their race or color.

Religious intolerance is the black reflection of a stupid prejudiced mind. Hate your neighbor today because his religious beliefs differ from yours and you lay the foundation for the next war, for which the blood of your sons must pay.

Walk upright and fearless toward a new day of religious understanding — a new day when all men shall respect each other's religious convictions. You will then face a new world opportunity. Look toward the hills beyond — the hills of peace — the blessings of the morning sun and your shadows of doubt will fall behind you.

Index

PUBLISHER'S NOTE

It would be quite impossible to index satisfactorily the wealth of homespun philosophy with which the author has enriched this volume. The reminiscences of pioneer farm life, with which he has illustrated his practical suggestions, present a similar problem. So we list below the chapters which dwell particularly on these subjects.

PHILOSOPHY

REMINISCENCE

Index

Chapter Titles are set ALL CAPITALS

www.ingramcontent.com/pod-product-compliance
Lightning Source LLC
Chambersburg PA
CBHW081131090426

42737CB00018B/3290